HAVANESE

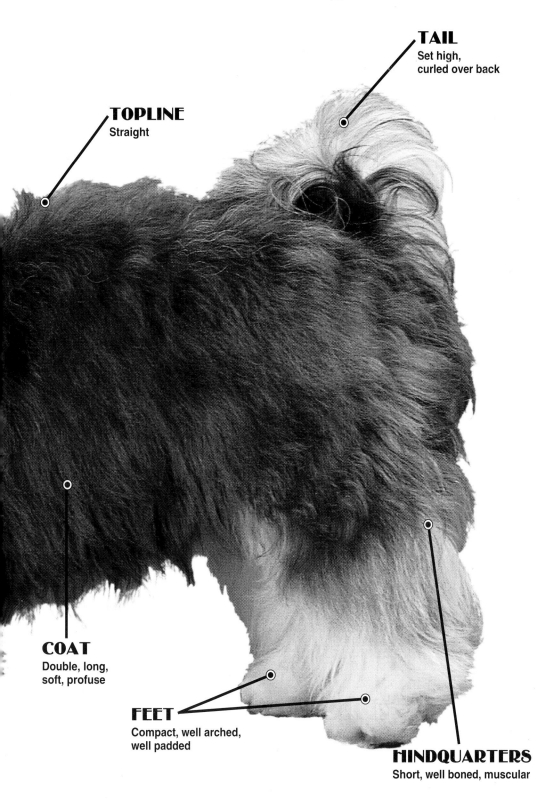

TAIL
Set high,
curled over back

TOPLINE
Straight

COAT
Double, long,
soft, profuse

FEET
Compact, well arched,
well padded

HINDQUARTERS
Short, well boned, muscular

Title Page: UKC Havana's Montrose Son, owned by Barbara Bogart.

Photographers: Vivian Becella, Barbara Bogart, Paulette Braun, Benay Brotman, Kay Burton, Jennifer Clark, Candy Derrick-Houston, Isabelle Francais, Dorothy Goodale, Alison Hashmall, Havana Doll House, Angela Houston, Darnell Phillips, Maxine Polansky, John and Sharon Shearman, Ricardo and Isabel Valenzuela

DEDICATION

This book is dedicated to the memory of my husband, Bert Goodale, the most patient husband in the universe, who supported and shared my dream to restore this rare breed to the former glory that it enjoyed in its native land of Cuba.

ACKNOWLEDGMENT

My deepest appreciation to my dear friend Joseph "Toli" Jemenez for all of the translations and research he assisted me with. My sincere thanks to my friend Sandy Schneider for allowing me to incorporate her wonderful "click and treat" training methods in this book. My everlasting gratitude to my wise and dear friend Sister Helen Reynolds, who kept me focused on my goal and without whose encouragement I could never have written the story about my years with the Havanese. My thanks also to Kris Steffeck for her grooming techniques incorporated herein and for typing the manuscript for this book.

© T.F.H. Publications, Inc.

Distributed in the UNITED STATES to the Pet Trade by T.F.H. Publications, Inc., 1 TFH Plaza, Neptune City, NJ 07753; on the Internet at www.tfh.com; in CANADA by Rolf C. Hagen Inc., 3225 Sartelon St., Montreal, Quebec H4R 1E8; Pet Trade by H & L Pet Supplies Inc., 27 Kingston Crescent, Kitchener, Ontario N2B 2T6; in ENGLAND by T.F.H. Publications, PO Box 74, Havant PO9 5TT; in AUSTRALIA AND THE SOUTH PACIFIC by T.F.H. (Australia), Pty. Ltd., Box 149, Brookvale 2100 N.S.W., Australia; in NEW ZEALAND by Brooklands Aquarium Ltd., 5 McGiven Drive, New Plymouth, RD1 New Zealand; in SOUTH AFRICA by Rolf C. Hagen S.A. (PTY.) LTD., P.O. Box 201199, Durban North 4016, South Africa; in JAPAN by T.F.H. Publications. Published by T.F.H. Publications, Inc.

MANUFACTURED IN THE
UNITED STATES OF AMERICA
BY T.F.H. PUBLICATIONS, INC.

HAVANESE

A COMPLETE AND RELIABLE HANDBOOK

Dorothy Goodale

RX-147

CONTENTS

INTRODUCTION

OUR AMAZING HAVANESE

Whenever I have occasion to take one of my little Havanese with me, invariably people will stop me and ask, "What kind of dog is that?" When I answer, "A Havanese," they then inquire, "What is a Havanese?" The editorial that I wrote so many years ago when I served as editor of the Havanese Club newsletter comes again to mind. Even today, it is still the best description of a Havanese that I know:

"What is a Havanese" you ask me?

"He is the light of my life, the sun in my morning, the most charming and discreet of beggars at my table. He will play the clown when I am sad . . . never failing to charm the smile right out of me. He is the ear when I need to tell something that I can trust with no other. He will dance for me, talk to me, be my most enthusiastic traveling companion with the most exemplary of manners. His personality has as many facets as a priceless gem. What more can I say? He is a Havanese!"

The Havanese is truly one of the most delightful of the small breeds. They are exceptionally intelligent and quick-witted. Obedience training is achieved with very little effort. Fast to learn and anxious to please, they are a charming, open-hearted breed with nothing sly or mean in their makeup. They thrive on affection and human companionship and are at their very best when participating as members of the family. They love children and will play tirelessly with them at any game. Havanese are powerful swimmers and love playing in the water, diving in and out like tiny seals.

In the same fashion they arrived in Cuba, some would return to Europe by way of the Italian ships, as some trading of the breed's offspring took place back and forth between the owners. After they arrived back on the European continent, they were often used as entertainers in the traveling circuses because of their keen intelligence and their love of the attention that comes from their adorable little "show-off" nature.

7

They are curious and busy constantly. They are good watchdogs, making sure to alert you when a visitor arrives, and then take their cue from you and welcome the guest when all seems well with the master. They are courageous and fearless in the face of danger. As they grow older, they become a bit standoffish with strangers, preferring to make friends with the visitor on their own terms and in their own time.

Well, where did the Havanese come from, you ask? Where has he been all of these years? This book will tell you about the history and introduce you to the nature of this little rare breed from Cuba.

Exceptionally intelligent and quick-witted, the Havanese is truly one of the most delightful of small breeds. Havana's Luna Pequeno, "Mooney," owned by Dorothy Goodale.

HISTORY OF THE HAVANESE

The exact origin of the Havanese is shrouded in the mists of antiquity. There are as many opinions as there are authors. However, all seem to agree that they must have originated in the Mediterranean area. Centuries ago, they were found in the southern parts of France, Italy, and Spain. Through extensive research I have come to the conclusion that perhaps all members of the Bichon group as we know them today were one type of small white dog from that

Although the exact origin of the Havanese is unknown, most experts agree that the breed originated in the western Mediterranean area and that its ancestors were brought to foreign shores by their owners. Puppies from The Goodale Kennel, Havana Doll House.

area. They were probably more like the smaller Bolognese of today, as the Bolognese cousin appears to have remained in his homeland all of these centuries. Their other cousins, depending on where they were carried by their owners or dispatched as gifts to other shores, were developed to resemble the type that pleased the owner, much in the same way that the small terriers of the British Isles were developed and changed by the land barons who owned them centuries ago.

When author Fiorenzo Fiorone wrote the book, *308 Recognized Breeds*, he stated that the Havanese was a descendant of the Italian Bolognese, which was taken by the Italians to Argentina and crossed with a small South American Poodle, creating a new member of the Bichon family. The hypothesis advanced by Dechamber is different. He believes the Havanese is descended from the Maltese, which at one time also came in various colors as the Havanese does today. He believes that the Havanese was brought to the West Indies by Spaniards and was at the time called the "Havana Silk Dog." In the *Encyclopedia of Dogs*, by Jones and Hamilton, it is written that the breed came originally from the western Mediterranean area

Cubans seem to believe that the Havanese was first brought to their homeland by Italian sea captains who carried them on board their ships for entertainment and trade. These exotic Toy dogs soon became known as Havanese, probably named for their port of entry in Havana. Havana's Mojito, owned by Ricardo and Isabel Valenzuela.

and that its ancestors traveled to Cuba during the days of the Spanish Empire.

In spite of all this history, the Cubans seem to feel that these little dogs were first brought to their shores by the Italian sea captains who carried them on board for entertainment and to further their personal trade. Upon docking in a port, the captain would dispatch his first mate to the home of one of the wealthy señoras bearing one of these darling, ribbon-bedecked, little dogs as an entree gift. The señora would then invite the captain and his first mate to dine in her home, affording the captain the opportunity to display and sell the rich contraband he had picked up in the exotic ports on his journey. This would be his profit aside from the cargo he carried for the company he sailed for. You might even say these fellows were possibly the first "moonlighters" in the business world. These little dogs soon became known as Havanese, probably named for the large port in Havana.

Havanese, like their ancestors, were becoming extinct when smuggled out of Cuba by their families fleeing their homeland at the time of the Great Exodus. Two of the families that brought their little dogs with them were the Perez family and the Fantasio family, who, combining their efforts, endeavored to preserve the breed from extinction. These were the first Havanese on record in the US. The cause for their near extinction transpired during the time of the Great Exodus as many families, thinking they would be returning in a very short time, felt secure in leaving their little pets in the care of housekeepers and servants. To try to smuggle them out became almost impossible, due to the lack of space aboard the departing ships. They never dreamed they were leaving their little pets, never again to be reunited.

A legend has been told that the most dedicated and enthusiastic defender of these little dogs was a Cuban lady named Catalina Lasa. Catalina was renowned for her beauty. She might well be called the Grand Dam of the Havanese breed. Her husband was a wealthy sugar baron from one of the most prominent Cuban families. The legend goes on to say that she loved these tiny dogs and felt they should be protected, and that she presented many to her wealthy friends as gifts. It was looked upon as a status symbol to own these little ambassadors from Italy. For the most part, these little dogs were seen only in the fine homes and country estates of the Cuban elite.

THE LEGEND OF A ROMANTIC TRAGEDY

"Old world" Cuba was changing rapidly around the turn of the century. The overthrow of Spanish domination and World War I brought many changes to Cuba. A government controlled by Spain was driven from Cuba by Teddy Roosevelt and his Rough Riders, ending 400 years of Spanish empire. The Treaty of Paris, which ended that war, established Cuba as an independent republic, at least for a period of time before a series of dictators took command of the government.

Opposite: In "old world" Cuba, it was looked upon as a status symbol to own a Havanese. These little dogs were seen only in the finest homes and country estates of the Cuban elite.

Cuba joined the allies in World War I and great increases in US investments made the tiny nation very dependent on its neighbors to the north. At the same time, it made some Cubans, as well as their American allies, very prosperous. Cuba was becoming a rich tourist playground. The horseless carriage was becoming the popular mode of travel, and US investors were building gambling casinos everywhere, as well as factories that paid very low wages to the working class. Sugar was still the king crop, but the sudden drop in prices brought other Cuban resources into focus, such as tobacco, coffee, and cattle. Cuba was beginning to manifest a classic case of "the rich get richer and the poor get poorer." Thus was the overall view of Cuba about the time a new star appeared on the horizon. This bright point of light in the heavens was the beautiful Catalina Lasa, the legend and the patron of our little breed, the Havanese. The little dog had existed in Cuba for many years, but there had never been a real devotion to the breed or a protective interest until Catalina took it under her wing and became its protector and patron. This renowned beauty was also destined to shake the very foundations of Cuba's high society as no other woman before her time had ever done. Catalina was a rare beauty from one of the impoverished aristocratic families. She married into one of the wealthiest and most successful families in Cuba. Her husband was one of the most powerful sugar barons of the time. His family was very jealous of Catalina's beauty and popularity, and in many subtle ways, never let her forget that they considered her beneath their station in society, and everything she had she owed to their generosity.

Catalina loved the little dogs and was devoted to them. They were her one happiness. She shared them as gifts with her wealthy friends, of which there

The romantic legend of Catalina Lasa, the beautiful Cuban baroness who became known as the protector and patron of the Havanese, is renowned in Cuba. Her devotion to the breed saved it from near extinction during the Great Exodus. Carousel's Sydney-Anne, owned by Darnell Phillips.

were many that loved and admired her. In spite of all this opulence, she was not really happy, and as you have probably already guessed, it was inevitable that one day she would meet the love of her life. He was another of the prosperous sugar barons of the time and even more prosperous than her husband. His name was Juan Pedro Baro. As their love for one another grew, they secretly planned to flee Cuba. In those days, in spite of all the modern changes, Cuba was still a strong Catholic state and this sort of thing was against the law. Even the Archbishop, having heard a whisper of the gossip, paid a visit to Catalina to point out the folly of her ways and to try to dissuade her from making a great mistake and bringing shame and disgrace to her husband's family. In spite of all the council, the love affair grew, and when her husband's family sought to bring charges against her, the lovers fled the country and sailed to France. They had friends in Paris and felt they would help them.

The scandal was the highlight of Cuban gossip for almost a decade. Even in Paris, stories of their indiscretions followed them. It was common knowledge that her rich and powerful mother-in-law wanted Catalina's head for leaving her son in what she felt was disgrace.

The story is told that at one point Catalina and Baro attended the opera and when they arrived and entered the theater, all the other patrons rose and left their seats. Nonetheless, the actors continued the opera to its finish, and when the curtain came down and raised again for the final bow, Catalina, in her gratitude for the actors' courtesy, tossed her valuable bracelets, necklaces, and other jewelry upon the stage for the actors, and the floor was covered with her gems and pearls.

Even in what they felt would be a haven, their indiscretions had followed them, and once more charges were brought against them. They found themselves forced to flee. Their plans were formed, and Catalina, disguised as a peasant girl, crossed the Alps into Italy. Baro, disguised as a seaman, boarded a sailing ship and also headed for Italy. Their plans were to meet again on the Bridge of Sighs in Venice. Their escape was successful, and they were reunited at the bridge. Baro, using his money and influence, sought an audience with the Pope. In Rome, the Pope, after listening to Catalina's story, granted her an annulment and personally married the lovers. With great joy, they were welcomed back to Paris by their friends where they honeymooned. They made plans to return to Cuba. Here again, they were enthusiastically welcomed by their friends who loved them and had supported them through their ordeal. Catalina became somewhat of a celebrity, as she was the first woman in Cuba to be granted a divorce. For a time they lived an idyllic life in a grand mansion that Baro bought for Catalina. Before long, Baro was appointed Cuban ambassador to France, and again they made plans to set sail for the France that they both had learned to love almost as much as their homeland.

Catalina must have brought some of her little dogs with her when they returned to Paris. It is recorded that one of these Havanese, Poulka, a little tobacco-brown female owned by a Madam Malenfer, won first prize when shown at one of Paris' first canine shows held at the Tuileries Gardens.

Catalina and her husband loved Paris, and they were caught up and welcomed into the hearts of high society. Baro commissioned a famous French horticulturist to develop a rose that would be named for Catalina. It was a brilliant orange shading to a lovely yellow throat. It was named the Catalina Rose. To this day in Cuba, a manifestation of enduring love is to present your sweetheart with a bouquet of Catalina roses.

The gods smiled upon the couple for a brief and idyllic time, and then one evening while dining at the famous Ritz Hotel in Paris, Catalina was served some mushrooms that later were proven to be poisonous, and in hours, she was dead.

Baro, needless to say, was quite mad with grief. He sought out the most prominent French scientist to oversee the embalming of her body and then decided to return his love to her homeland. So, with Catalina lying in state surrounded by her namesake roses and black candles, the mourning ship departed France's shores bearing all-black sails and flags, and the tragic, ill-fated lovers once more sailed for Cuba.

In Cuba, Baro commissioned the building of a beautiful mausoleum for his love. It was constructed of the lovely pink marble they both had so much admired on their visit to Italy. He also commissioned the famous French crystal artisan, Rene Lalique, to design crystal panel inserts to be placed within the mausoleum, so that when a certain light struck them through the windows, there was created a light so brilliant that it was blinding. This magnificent structure erected for his love stands near the entrance to the Cemetery of Colon in a rather private little park area, and although many of the cemetery statues and other mausoleums have been vandalized, Catalina's stands intact as the day she was laid to rest there.

Because I have a good reason to be a romantic, my eyes mist when I think of her, this beautiful lady with her short sad life. We remember that, through her love

The first Havanese on record in the US were smuggled out of Cuba by families fleeing their homeland. Two of the families that brought their dogs with them were the Perez and Fantasio families; their combined efforts helped to preserve the breed.

Tracing the Havanese's lines back to the foundation stock, it is believed that the original dog was white and that breeds were later added to develop color. Pablo Ricky De ZB's, owned by Angela Houston.

and caring protection, she bestowed a gift on us that we treasure to this day—our little Havanese.

THE FOUNDATION STOCK

For those of you who are tracing your Havanese's lines back to the foundation stock, I have included the lines of the foundation dogs.

What we discovered over the years and found most interesting was that in the breeding, it was easier to get back to white than any other color, and all of the dark colors tend to fade and "grizzle" out as the dog gets older. This observation led us to believe that possibly, in the beginning, the original dog was white and breeds were added to develop color. Personally, I still prefer the white. A small, well-groomed, white dog with expressive dark eyes and a dark nose is an absolute "stand out," and strangely enough, the white dogs tend to have slightly wavy coats, while most of the dark colors tend to have different degrees of curliness—almost as though the color and the curl are gene linked. I am convinced the original dog was white, bearing out the conviction they came from the Bichon group in the Mediterranean area.

Several years ago, Cathy Flamholtz, the author of the now renowned books, *Celebration of Rare Breeds*

I and II, told me a very interesting story. She told me of having the opportunity to meet a very elderly Cuban lady in Miami. The lady's family had been very wealthy, but they lost everything when they escaped the island in the first Cuban airlift.

She told of several delightful dogs she had owned years before in Cuba. Cathy, with her love for dogs, was fascinated by these stories and took several dog books to her home. The Cuban woman patiently looked over the photos. She thought the Bichon Frise was similar but not quite "it." Finally, Cathy took a very old and rare book to her and she clapped her hands with joy when she saw the photo of the Bolognese. Cathy said she wished she would have had a photo of a white Havanese—surely this must have been the dog she remembered so fondly.

The "Perez/Fantasio" Line
SIRE: Silver Tiger (Silver)
Show Girl (Black/White Trim; 9-plus in.; 9 lbs)
DAM: Rags Girl (Chocolate)

SIRE: Silver Tiger (Silver)
Inky Doll (Black; 10 in.; 10 lbs)
DAM: Rags Girl (Chocolate)

SIRE: Silver Tiger (Silver)
Dark Lady (Black; 9-plus in.; 10-plus lbs)
DAM: Rags Girl (Chocolate)

SIRE: Silver Tiger (Silver)
Buttons 'n Bows (Black & White; 9-plus in.;
10-plus lbs)
DAM: Rags Girl (Chocolate)

SIRE: Tigre Luna (White)
Carmalita (Gold w/White Trim; 9 in.; 9 lbs)
DAM: Bella (Gold)

SIRE: Fancy Pants (Cream/Silver)
Silver Promise (Silver; 10-plus in.; 11 lbs)
DAM: Mimi (Black/White Party Mix)

SIRE: Jefe Pequeno (From Barba's Line)
Tigre Luna
DAM: Nieve (From Barba's Line)
Most consistent sires from size and type.
Most of our whites came from his siring.

The "Barba" Line

SIRE: Negro Pajaro (Black/Silver)
Nieve (Light Silver w/White Trim; 10 in.; 11 lbs)
DAM: Amapolita Adorado (White)

SIRE: Negro Pajaro (Black/Silver)
Querido (Black w/White Trim; 9-plus in.; 10 lbs)
DAM: Amapolita Adorado (White)

SIRE: Negro Pajaro (Black/Silver)
Dulce (White w/Champagne Trim; 10 in.; 10 lbs)
DAM: Elena Blanca (White)

SIRE: Negro Palaro (Black/Silver)
Sorpresa (Cream w/Gold Ears; 10-plus in.; 11 lbs)
DAM: Elena Blanca (White)

SIRE: Rey David (Champagne)
Jefe Pequeno (White/Champagne; 10 in.; 11 lbs)
DAM: Botines Bella (Cream)
Quita and Pansey did not produce.
[Ezequiel Barba's Original Pedigrees]

THE HAVANESE ORGANIZATION

After working with the Havanese for about five years and having given up hope of discovering any more Havanese in the US, we decided the time had come for an organization to unify the Havanese and their breeders. The year was 1974.

Havana's Tigre Luna, owned by Dorothy Goodale, is one of Havana Doll House's foundation sires.

The most enthusiastic fanciers were called together to offer suggestions and volunteer as officers
of this new club. First, a name was decided upon. It
was to be The Bichon Havanais Fanciers Club of
America. This struck us as a bit long, but nonetheless,
very impressive for this unique little breed. Unfortunately, at that time we were unaware that before a few
years had passed, this name was to cause confusion
and misunderstandings with the Bichon Frise owners.
Many were under the impression that we were cross-
ing some unknown breed with their little Bichon Frise
and creating a new breed.

After several irate breeders had contacted us, we
decided to seek professional council. At that time it was
still not a well-known fact that there were several
breeds in Europe that carried the name Bichon in
conjunction with their breed name. In fact, there are
five different Bichon groups, all related centuries ago,
but now recognized as different breeds. The Bichon
Frise was just coming into focus in the US, and I'm sure
that most of the owners were unaware of the fact that
the name "Bichon" was used widely in Europe—Bichon
actually meaning "small lap dog." The Bichon group
that had arrived previously to the Bichon Frise had long
since dropped the Bichon as a prefix and were merely
called Maltese. Upon professional council, we decided
to also drop the Bichon word and use the American
spelling and pronunciation of the word, Havanese.
After a call for a membership vote the club name
became The Havanese Fanciers Club of America.

At our first meeting in 1974, officers were voted into
office and their duties respectfully assigned. A consti-
tution and by-laws were written and approved by the
board, and I set up a registry to keep official records
and lineage on all Havanese in the US up to that date.
We decided on the format for our registrations and
these were sent out to all owners. That spring of 1974,
our club was born.

In our club's infancy, all paperwork was conducted
free of charge, but as the cost of paper, printing, and
postage mounted, we came to an early conclusion that
charges would have to be assessed for registrations,
memberships, and most paperwork. However, all
charges were kept to a minimum. I wrote to the European
FCI for the official standard for the Havanese and this
standard was adopted as our official standard.

I volunteered to print out a newsletter every other
month to inform our membership of all developments

and encouraged members to write in with news of their Havanese or any other information that would be of interest to all of us. In no time at all, the club became an extended family with members beginning to really know each other, offering encouragement and knowledge to all.

As the years passed and the club grew, there were many changes, but change is good and change means progress. Our breed and its club flourished. I am happy and very proud to have been a part of those early beginnings.

For more information, contact your local breed club or the kennel clubs in your country. In the UK, contact Havanese Club of Great Britain, Mrs. C. Alcock, 49 Berkeley Rd., Coventry CV5 6NY, England.

Barbara Bogart, president of The Original Havanese Club, with three of her beloved Havanese.

STANDARD FOR THE HAVANESE

DESCRIPTION OF THE BREED

The Havanese is considered one of the Bichon Group, which consists of five distinct breeds: the Bichon Maltese; the Bichon Bolognese; the Bichon Havanais (Havanese); the Bichon Tenerife (Frise); and the Coton de Tulear. They are nonshedding and odorless, and their soft coat is easily kept with frequent brushing, combing, and periodic bathing. The coat ranges from soft and wavy to curly. Both coats are correct, but for ease of maintenance in full length, the slightly wavy is preferred. Many owners find that the curly coats are easier to keep neat by shortening them. The breed standard states, however, that the

According to the standard, the Havanese is a sturdy, short-legged, small dog, with a soft, profuse, untrimmed coat, and a plumed tail curled over his back. Havana's Tickles My Funny Bone, owned by Dorothy Goodale.

Havanese is to be shown in the show ring in "natural" coat length. There are various colors and several shades of each coat. The colors range from white through shades of cream, champagne, gold, chocolate, silver, blue, sable, and black, or any combination of these colors; pure white being perhaps the rarest.

The eyes are large and dark, with a lovely soft expression, and the deep pigmented halos around the eyes accentuate the size and expression. The muzzle is neither sharp nor blunt, with a moderate stop. The nose and lips are black, except on the true chocolate colored dog and then the pigment will be brown. The true chocolate Havanese often has lighter eyes.

The body is long compared to the height. The ribs are well sprung. They are very muscular and strong for their small stature. Their gait is lively with a bit of a spring to it. Their weight ranges from 7 to 13 pounds, and they are considered a toy breed. When in motion, there is an air of jauntiness that is unmistakable about them.

The following is the official standard for the Havanese as approved and accepted by the American Kennel Club.

OFFICIAL STANDARD FOR THE HAVANESE

General Appearance—The Havanese is a sturdy, short-legged small dog with a soft profuse, untrimmed coat. His plumed tail is carried curled over his back. He is an affectionate, happy dog with a lively, springy gait.

Size, Proportion, Substance—The height ranges from 8 to 11 1/2 inches, the ideal being 9 to 10 1/2 inches. The weight ranges from 7 to 13 pounds, the ideal being 8 to 11 pounds. Any dog whose weight deviates greatly from the stated range is a major fault. *Any dog measuring under 8 or over 11 inches is a disqualification.* The body from the chest to the buttocks is longer than the height at the shoulders and should not appear to be square. Forelegs and hindlegs are relatively short, but with sufficient length to set the dog up so as not to be too close to the ground. The Havanese is a sturdy dog, and while a small breed, is neither fragile nor overdone.

Head—Medium length proportionate to the size of the body. *Eyes* are large, almond shaped and very dark with a gentle expression. In the blue and silver coat shades, eyes may be a slightly lighter color; in chocolate coat shades, the eyes may be a lighter color. However,

Opposite: An affectionate, happy dog, with a lively, springy gait, the Havanese is known for his love of attention and "show-off" nature. Havana's Sunshine, "Happy," owned by Benay Brotman.

the darker eye is preferred. Eye rims are black for all colors except chocolate shaded coats, whose eye rims are self-colored. Small or round eyes; broken or insufficient pigment on the eye rim(s) are *faults*. Wild, bulging or protruding eyes a *major fault. Total absence of pigment on one or both eye rims is a disqualification. Ears* are set neither too high nor too low and are dropped, forming a gentle fold and covered with long feathering. They are slightly raised, moderately pointed, neither fly-away nor framing the cheeks. *Skull* is broad and somewhat rounded with a moderate stop. The cheeks are flat and the lips clean. The length of the *muzzle* is equal to the distance to the stop to the back of the occiput. The muzzle is neither snipey nor blunt. *Nose and lips* are solid black on all colors except the true chocolate dog, whose nose and lips are solid, self-colored brown. *Dudley nose, nose and lips other than black, except the solid, self-colored brown on the true chocolate dog are disqualifications.* Scissors bite preferred; a level bite is permissible. Full dentition of incisors preferred for both upper and lower jaws. Crooked or missing teeth are *faults*. Overshot or undershot bite, wry mouth are *major faults*.

Considered a Toy breed, the Havanese's height can range from 8 to 11 1/2 inches and their weight can range from 7 to 13 pounds. Pablo Ricky De ZB's, owned by Angela Houston.

Neck, Topline, Body—*Neck* of moderate length, neither too long nor too short. *Topline* is straight with a very slight rise over the croup. *Flanks* are well raised. *Ribs* well rounded. *Tail* is set high, carried

curled over the back and plumed with long silky hair. While standing, a dropped tail is permissible.

Forequarters—*Forelegs* are well boned and straight, the length from the elbow to the withers equal to the distance from the foot to the elbow. Dewclaws may be removed. *Feet* are compact, well arched, well padded. Any foot turning in or out is a *fault*.

Hindquarters—*Legs* are relatively short, well boned and muscular with moderate angulation; straight when viewed from the rear. Dewclaws may be removed. *Feet* are same as front feet. Fault is same as the front feet.

Coat—The Havanese is a double-coated breed with soft hair, both in outer and undercoat. The hair is very long and profuse, shown completely natural. The coat type ranges from straight to curly, the wavy coat being preferred. The curly coat is allowed to cord. The adult coat reaches a length of 6 to 8 inches. No preference shall be given to a dog with an excessively profuse or long coat. Short hair on all but puppies is a *fault*. It is permissible to braid the hair on each side of the head above the eyes, but the coat may not be parted down the middle of the back. No scissoring of the hair on the top of the head is allowed, nor trimming or neatening of the coat of any kind permitted except for the feet which may be neatened to avoid the appearance of "boat" or "slipper" feet. *Coat trimmed in any way except for neatening at the feet is a disqualification.* All colors, ranging from pure white to shades of cream, champagne, gold, black, blue, silver, chocolate or any combination of these colors including parti and tri. No preference is given to one color over another.

Gait—The gait is unique and "springy" which accentuates the happy character of the Havanese. The forelegs reach straight and forward freely from the shoulder with the hind legs converging toward a straight line. The tail is carried up over the back when gaiting. Hackney gait, paddling, moving too close in the rear, and tail not carried over the back when gaiting are *faults*.

Temperament—Affectionate, happy.

DISQUALIFICATIONS

Any dog under 8 1/2 or over 11 1/2 inches. Total absence of pigment on one or both eye rims. Dudley nose, nose and lips other than black, except for the solid, self-colored brown on the true chocolate dog. Coat trimmed in any way except for neatening at the feet.

Approved: June 1995
Effective: February 1, 1996

Opposite: The Havanese is a double-coated breed, with soft hair in both the outercoat and undercoat. The hair is very long and profuse, and coat type ranges from straight to curly, with the wavy coat being preferred. Sidney, owned by Vivian Becella.

YOUR NEW HAVANESE PUPPY

BRINGING YOUR PUPPY HOME

Your puppy will look to you for the comfort and protection he felt with his mother and littermates. Everything is new to him, so he may not be very frisky and playful at first. He must have time to get acquainted. Too much fondling and petting will only confuse him, so let him make his own advances. It may take a few days before he feels completely at home. Treat him gently—loud noises, sudden grabs, etc. can frighten puppies, and he can be permanently injured by rough handling, both physically and mentally.

Always lift the puppy by placing one hand under his chest and the other under his hindquarters. Never pick him up by the scruff of his neck or let him dangle. Teach children in the household how to lift him. Better yet, encourage young children to sit on the floor and play with the puppy rather than picking him up. Remind them that the puppy is not a plaything but will be their playmate after they have won his confidence.

If the puppy has been sent from afar and arrives in a crate, he will very likely be nervous and upset by his trip. If he needs it, clean him off with a damp cloth. If you take him home from the airport in your car, hold him in your lap or close to your side so he won't jounce about. Take along a soft towel to spread in your lap so that you will be prepared for drooling or carsickness. Talk to him in cheerful tones on the trip home.

Have a place ready for him. His bed should be draft proof and should be a box, basket, or crate put in an out-of-the-way place where he can feel secure and observe some of the household activity. Do not confine him to a place where he will be lonely, such as a

28

basement or garage. Havanese must be part of the family. Put a little fence of some sort around his corner of the room (a playpen that is secure is the best) with newspapers spread on the floor. He'll have enough exploring to do there.

Respect the puppy's right to be undisturbed whenever he seeks his bed for a rest and when he is eating his meals. Talk to him. He won't understand a word at this point, but your friendly tone of voice will help to give him confidence. He will be irresponsible, just like a baby, for some time to come, but you can set the pattern of his life so he will thrive and grow and learn.

It is also a good idea to place his crate up on a chair next to your bed the first few nights to console the puppy, because he will miss his littermates at first. If he is confined to his crate at night he cannot soil the carpet of the bedroom and still will feel near you. Tap lightly on the crate if he cries and gently tell him to "Hush" and "Go to sleep." The sound of your soft voice is usually enough to let him know he is not alone. Sometimes a hot water bottle in his bedding or the ticking of a clock under his blanket will soothe him to sleep.

On his first night in his new home, your little Havanese may be missing the company of his mother and littermates. Giving him some extra attention will help him to overcome his loneliness.

If he is really putting up a fuss, it is possible that he needs to go out again, so it might be wise to take him to his special place where you want him to eliminate. You do not want to force him to soil his crate. A dog that has gotten used to sitting in his feces becomes a very

It is important that everyone in the household learns to hold a fragile puppy the proper way. Always lift your Havanese pup by placing one hand under his chest and the other under his hindquarters. Six-week-old Havana's Osito.

dirty dog, and the habit may be hard to break. Then again, you really don't want to make a habit of getting up each night. You want him to learn to sleep through the night, so if this occurs, try feeding him a bit earlier at night and taking him out for the last time a little later. I cannot stress enough that dogs are truly creatures of habit, so keep in mind always with your program of training that this is the habit you wish to instill.

SLEEP HABITS

It is a good idea to start the new puppy off in his own bed. Make sure that he is confined to his crate or bed in such a way that he cannot get out in the night and get lost and chilled. No matter how well heated a home is, there are always drafts along the floors at night. Wicker baskets and foam filled beds will encourage chewing and cause digestive problems. His crate or playpen serves as an ideal place for him to sleep or be confined in while you must be away from him or during the night. An old sweater or robe that you no longer use and that you have recently worn will often comfort him in the night now that he is separated from his littermates.

For the first few nights, his crate should be kept close to your bed where you can speak to him to comfort him if he whimpers. Later, and during the daytime, provide a place your puppy can call his own. House dogs that stay inside most of the day develop a lighter coat and need to sleep in a warm, dry place away from drafts. A word of caution: Keep you dog's bed away from radiators, stoves, and heat registers, because artificial heat tends to dry the skin. Wherever your dog sleeps, by all means, see that his bedding is cleaned often. At this point, once more, I would like to say that Havanese are odorless and nonshedding and are truly at their best indoors as a full-fledged member of the family.

TOYS

Puppies love to chew on old socks tied in knots. Gumabone® and Nylabone® toys help keep the teeth clean and the gums healthy. Be very careful when buying commercial pet toys and make sure that they do not contain bells, squeakers, or metal parts that can be chewed off and choke the puppy.

TEETH

Your puppy will cut his adult teeth when he is four to five months old. Usually this happens without any problems, but occasionally a "baby" tooth refuses to be dislodged by the incoming adult tooth. The baby tooth must be removed or the other teeth may be permanently misaligned. Check the puppy's mouth frequently during this time. Sturdy chew toys will help remove loose teeth. If a tooth is being retained, have your veterinarian attend to it. Don't attempt tooth extraction yourself.

HOME ALONE

First, prepare a playpen to confine the puppy in until he is housetrained. This could be an exercise pen from a dog supply catalog or pet shop or a plastic pen from a department store. My favorite is a playpen that consists of smooth plastic poles about two inches apart. They cannot be chewed through, climbed, or jumped out of. It also has the advantage over all the others because it has an easy-to-clean floor. This pen measures four feet by four feet and is two feet tall. Don't even for a moment entertain the idea of a barricade at the kitchen door. To a puppy's little ingenious mind, it merely presents a challenge that will keep him focused until you find the little fellow is in the living room sleeping in the recliner upon your arrival home.

Get him some safe toys to keep him entertained while you are at work. Chew toys are favorites—puppies spend a great deal of time chewing when they are bored and it is better that they chew their possessions rather than yours.

Remove the door from his little crate so that it doesn't close keeping him from his napping place. Place it in his playpen along with his food and water bowls. Keep these on one side of the playpen and cover the other side with newspapers. The puppy will try to get as far from his bed as possible when nature calls. Put an old sweatshirt or something you have worn and no longer use in the crate for his bedding. Your individual scent will comfort him in your absence.

Divide his toys in three selections and each day pick up one group and replace it with one of the other two sets. In doing this, his toys always look fairly new and interesting to him as you rotate them each day. Keep a few in the freezer. These will help while he is cutting teeth.

Leave a radio playing on a station that is not all

Have a place ready for your Havanese when he arrives. His bed should be put in an out of the way spot where he can feel secure but still observe household activity and feel like part of the family. PR Havana's Teddy Bear Burton, owned by Kay Burton.

music. Hearing voices will help to keep him from feeling he is all alone.

Now, about your "hellos" and "goodbyes." When saying goodbye, be sure he has been in the playpen for at least one-half hour so that he does not associate the pen with your departure. Do not talk to him in a sympathetic tone, or he will immediately guess something he is not going to like is about to happen. Keep your goodbyes casual. Toss him one of his freezer toys and just leave. You might try leaving him for short periods of time so that your first day back at work will not be too traumatic for both of you.

Like your goodbye, keep your hello just as casual. Lift him from his pen and go out to the yard (don't just put him out) and take him to his designated spot at the far corner of the yard. Use your selected command word and praise him lavishly when he succeeds. Now give him some prime playtime. This will be a crucial time for him and you want to give him the security of knowing you are always coming home and it will always be his fun time.

Try to manage a few short car rides to keep him used to traveling with you. See to it that he has an empty tummy for the trip by removing his food bowl at least two hours before starting. A full tummy will only make him carsick, and this will distress him and he will associate it with the car.

The most important hint of all is give loads of love, love, love.

SAFETY

The puppy should never be put on anything high and left unattended even for a minute. Havanese puppies have no fear of falling and will walk off into space and can be seriously injured. Stairwells should be blocked off at first, also. If you have an upstairs hall with a banistered section or the other side showing a drop off, cover this while the puppy is young enough to squeeze through the rungs and drop to the floor below.

Keep a firm hold on the puppy while carrying him. Puppies are very quick to wriggle from your arms. Only allow adults and older children to pick him up and carry him about. Encourage small children to sit on the floor and love the puppy rather than pick him up and carry him.

Do not leave the puppy where there are small openings that he can work his head into, or become caught in and be in danger of strangling. Puppies are

very curious little fellows, and it will be up to you to protect him from these dangers.

An important safety tip: Never leave your dog in a closed car. Every year many puppies and adult dogs left in closed cars die from heatstroke or lack of oxygen. In a very short time, the temperature inside a car rises alarmingly high. Even leaving the windows cracked does not solve the problem.

Make sure your dog is safely on a leash or in a secure area when outside. More dogs are killed each year by automobiles than by disease. There is really no excuse for this. It is a mockery to say that a dog cannot be happy unless allowed full freedom. We dare not allow our Havanese on the streets free to come and go as he pleases, if we desire him to live. Provide him with a fenced yard big enough to stretch his legs and he will be perfectly happy. Never give him a moment off the lead when you take him for walks, unless he is completely and totally obedience trained. Even then, it is very risky. That brief glimpse of the dog across the street might tempt him to forget all he has learned and go dashing out into traffic.

Getting accustomed to a new environment may be difficult for a young puppy. Care, kindness, and encouragement will make your pet feel confident and help him to become a well-adjusted adult.

THE THIRTEEN COMMANDMENTS OF PUPPY RAISING

First Commandment: When training your puppy, always apply praise and reward rather than punishment.

Second Commandment: When working with your puppy, always make eye contact first.

Third Commandment: When your puppy exhibits fear—no matter what the situation—never console him in sympathetic voice tones. Keep an upbeat cheerful tone.

Fourth Commandment: Never let your puppy have his own way when he is being demanding and/or bratty. This is rewarding him for bad behavior.

Fifth Commandment: Never leave a collar on your unattended puppy.

Sixth Commandment: Never leave your puppy in a closed, locked car during hot or extremely cold weather.

Seventh Commandment: Never give your puppy any kind of bones or rawhide. Give him safe toys like Nylabones® or Gumabones® instead.

Eighth Commandment: Never switch your puppy suddenly from one brand of food to another. This should be a gradual process.

Ninth Commandment: Never leave your puppy unattended in a swimming pool area.

Tenth Commandment: Never walk your puppy off lead no matter how well trained you think he is.

Eleventh Commandment: Do not feed your puppy within a three-hour period of taking him for a ride in the car if he has a problem with motion sickness. Try feeding when you get back home.

Twelfth Commandment: If you are crate training your puppy, never expect him to be contained in the crate for more than three hours without a break to go outside to his special place.

Thirteenth Commandment: Never allow your puppy to growl or snap over his food bowl or a toy.

The most important of any rule is to be sure to hug and praise and snuggle your puppy often. Enjoy him!

FEEDING YOUR HAVANESE

Havanese pups should have a bowl of dry feed, in addition to their water bowl, to nibble on free of choice throughout the day. Morning and night, I take some of this same dry feed and add enough warm water to soften the feed, and add some cottage cheese (do not mix the cottage cheese in with the feed—just put it to one side of the dish). A small dish of this combination is fed in the morning and evening. When you find that the puppy is eating more of the dry kibble than the "wet feed," gradually eliminate the "wet feed" and feed just the dry kibble. In most cases, if the dry feed is there in his bowl all day, the puppy will pace himself and not be an overeater. Dry food is much better for the puppy's teeth than the "wet feed" and is preferred as the puppy grows older. The cottage cheese becomes a treat from time to time after the transition to the dry kibble. Keep your puppy on puppy kibble until one year of age, then gradually switch to adult kibble.

Never leave wet feed standing after allowing a reasonable time for the puppy to eat. Take it away and don't feed again until you mix a fresh meal for the next feeding. Keep food and water dishes clean. Don't feed your puppy food that is too hot or too cold—make it lukewarm. Don't add too much liquid to the food, because it will become soggy. The amount of food to give puppies depends on your puppy's age, size, and activity. Also, some puppies assimilate their food better in the beginning than others. The amount that keeps one puppy round and solid may not be adequate for another puppy of the same age or even the same litter. The best guide is your own observation.

Never feed fresh fish, cooked or raw. Bones are also a no-no. Not only can they choke him, but splinters can pierce the stomach and intestines and cause internal bleeding. Dairy milk will cause a very loose stool and upset the puppy's stomach. Cow's milk is not at all the same as their mother's milk, and once weaned, they no longer need milk. Cottage cheese is an excellent substitute. Game meat of any kind, cooked or raw, can poison your puppy.

Do not feed the puppy just before a ride in the car. Puppies do get carsick. The motion may disturb him, so make his first trips short ones around the block or even let him get used to sitting in the car while it is standing still. If you get your puppy used to the car when he is young, he will be an excellent traveler. Feed him when you arrive home. If the pup has eaten and then gets carsick, he will connect the sickness with the car and he may never become a good traveler.

Good nutrition is imperative if you want your Havanese puppy to develop properly.

GROOMING YOUR HAVANESE

PUPPY GROOMING

Develop the habit of grooming your puppy every day or two. It will keep his coat clean and shiny. A little puppy doesn't have enough coat to make an issue of it, but if he learns to enjoy his grooming sessions when he is young, he will be much easier to handle when he really needs this care. Get him used to being put up on a low table or bench for grooming. Inspect his skin for eruptions, sores, fleas, or other parasites that you might have in your locality. Do have them treated properly. Many good powders and other commercial products are available to get rid of fleas or ticks, but be sure to use a kind recommended for puppies. Your puppy should have a thorough brushing and combing at least twice a week and more often if the coat is extremely heavy and/or long. This is accomplished by combing all of the hair with a backward sweep from tail

Develop the habit of grooming your Havanese puppy every day or two—it will keep his coat clean and shiny. Havana's Black Jack.

Having the proper tools will make grooming easier and more comfortable for your dog. Be sure to select the tools recommended for your particular breed.

to head using a medium-tooth steel comb and then smoothing it all back down the other way with a good stiff brush. The pup's nails should be kept short. Cutting just the tip off once a week will prevent cutting into the quick, which causes bleeding. If this is done consistently as a puppy, there will be no problem with nail cutting when he is grown. Keep the hair pulled out of the ear holes and keep the inside of the ear clean with a cotton swab. Do not clean any farther down than you can see.

Puppies do not often need baths because they are odorless. When necessary, use a commercial tearless shampoo that does not burn the eyes and a good commercial pet rinse that helps to prevent hair tangling. When you rinse your puppy off, hold the nose up high and just spray up to the nose taking care not to get water in it. This way he can breathe while being rinsed and will not fear the water. Always be sure your puppy or grown dog is completely dry before you allow him to run outdoors where he may become chilled. Blow dry and comb at the same time. Do not, under any circumstances, delegate the task of bathing the puppy to any child. This is definitely a job for an adult.

GROOMING TOOLS

These are the tools you will need for grooming your Havanese:

1. A medium soft slicker brush for the backhand brushing to the skin.

2. Cutting scissors for the neatening of all tag ends (do not use around eyes).

3. Flea comb for removing matter at the inside corners of the eyes.

4. Nail trimmers.

5. Medium-tooth comb to help in removing tangles and smoothing down the coat.

6. Nose scissors for trimming around eyes (be sure the ends are round).

7. A large pin brush, also for brushing down coat on finishing grooming.

8. A pair of good tweezers will also be helpful for pulling hair out of the ear holes.

GROOMING TIPS FOR BEGINNERS

Always use the proper equipment. Most beginners tend to overbuy equipment, so before you purchase haphazardly, select the proper tools as suggested for your breed.

Good grooming behavior should be taught to your dog at any early age and can be an enjoyable experience for both dog and owner, if you remember two basic rules:

1. Dogs learn by repetition, correction, and praise.

2. Dogs should associate grooming with a pleasant experience.

Good grooming behavior should be taught to your Havanese at an early age. Because dogs learn by repetition, putting him on a firm table each time you groom him will eventually teach him to behave during this daily procedure.

Use a firm table for grooming. Because dogs learn by repetition, put your pup on this table each time you brush or groom him. Eventually, your dog will learn that he must behave when he is being groomed. Never use an unsteady table. The dog will be frightened and try to jump off.

Make sure your grooming table has a nonslip rubber top. For your own comfort, invest in an adjustable grooming table so that you won't have to bend down so far to groom a small dog or stand on tiptoe to groom a large breed.

Do your grooming in a room with adequate lighting. Have light coming from above and behind you. Teach your dog to lie on his side while he is being brushed.

Don't expect your dog to stay perfectly still for hours on the grooming table when you first begin grooming. Dogs must be trained to behave on the table. Young puppies have short periods of concentration and will not stand still very long. If your puppy is very young, plan no more than 15 to 20 minutes of grooming at a time. A good way to begin table training is to stand the puppy on the table for brushing. Place your free hand under the stomach for support and to give the puppy confidence, then quickly run a brush through the coat. Speak quietly and reassuringly to the dog. At first, he may squirm about, but if you repeat this procedure every day for about two weeks, he will learn to stay still and behave.

It takes a great deal of time to brush out a long-coated show dog. If the dog learns to lie on his side, he can rest while being brushed, and you will find it easier to brush out the hair on the chest and the insides of the legs. If your dog is frightened by the sound of the clippers, hold him on your lap and rest the clippers near his back with the motor running. He will become accustomed to the noise.

When grooming, you must learn to be firm without being mean. Never hit your dog to make him behave on the grooming table. If his disobeys, correct him until he does what you want, then praise him. When correcting the dog, use a firm tone of voice and pick one word for correction, such as "Stop" or "No." Make sure you always use the same word so that your dog understands what you want him to do. Be consistent. Don't let your dog get away with something one day then reprimand him for doing the same thing the next day.

Toy dogs are very sensitive to the tones of human

voices. If you lose your patience, immediately stop whatever you are doing and take the dog off the table. Remember that the dog must not think of grooming as an unpleasant experience, so postpone the session until another time if you think you are losing control. Do not talk baby talk to the dog or play with him while he is on the grooming table. He is there to be groomed, not to play games. If he has been cooperative, reward him with a biscuit or treat when the grooming session is finished.

Limit the use of clippers or scissors on a dirty dog. This dulls equipment quickly. Scissors must be sharp and loose. Tight scissors prevent smooth scissoring. When scissoring near the vulva or testicles, place your free hand over them for protection. There is no excuse for nicking a dog's genitals. He will never forget it and will not cooperate the next time he is groomed.

Never cut out mats from the coat. If your dog is matted, follow the suggestions found in the brushing and coat problems section.

Follow this sequence each time you groom your dog:

1. Thoroughly brush and comb the dog to remove tangles and/or dead hair.

2. Clip toenails and clean ears.

3. Check skin for parasites.

4. Do any clipping or stripping work in the rough, if necessary.

5. Bathe and dry the dog. Apply cream rinse, tangle remover, or parasite treatment if necessary.

6. Do final clipping or stripping work.

7. Do any body and leg scissoring or thinning.

8. Finish head area last.

BRUSHING YOUR HAVANESE

1. Have your correct equipment assembled and a thick towel or small rug on your grooming table.

2. Place your Havanese on his side. At first, you may have to hold him there, talking gently but firmly to him until he is relaxed and calm.

3. With your brush, start with the back flank. Use smooth gentle strokes—always upward and away from the body. Brush the hair in layers, moving down and around the leg to the bottom of the foot. Do not move to the next layer until the brush is moving smoothly through the coat, indicating that all mats have been removed. Clean the dead hair often from

Grooming time should be enjoyable for both you and your Havanese. Short, cheerful sessions and a patient attitude are a must.

your brush with the medium-tooth comb.

4. If you come upon a mat that is large or particularly stubborn, treat it in the manner described in the following pages on mats. Remember always that you are trying to make this a fun time for you and your dog, so be gentle at all times.

5. Holding the back leg up, brush the hair on the stomach up to the front of the leg.

6. Go back to the brushed flank area and brush the body coat on the side up to the front leg.

7. Proceed to brushing the front leg in the same manner as the back leg—starting high on the shoulder and working down to the foot.

8. Turn the dog over and continue doing the opposite side in the same manner as the first side.

9. Stand the dog up with the rear toward you and brush the rear and tail. When brushing around the genital area, be sure to cover that area with your hand, as it would be quite painful to brush the area with the wire slicker brush.

10. Starting at the base of the tail, move up the center of the back making sure to overlap the side coat you brushed while the dog was on his side.

11. Brush the neck area and the armpits and look for any mats that tend to hide behind the ears.

12. Brush the ears—inside and out. This would also be the time to remove any hair from the ear hole. There is an antibiotic powder on the market that is just for this

purpose. Put a bit of powder in each ear. Massage and wait a few moments. Then be amazed at how easily the hair is removed with your fingers or tweezers.

13. With your flea comb or a cotton ball, carefully remove any matter from the inside corner of the eyes.

14. At this point, I really prefer to finish the grooming session with combing the face, beard, and head using the medium-tooth comb. Brushes around the eyes can cause a great deal of damage if the dog moves quickly into the path of the brush.

15. Trim just a bit off the toenails. If this is done a bit at a time each week, the quick of the nail will start to recede. You should be able, in time, to keep the nails short enough that you cannot hear them on a tile floor when the dog walks. Cutting into the quick is painful and can make your dog hard to control at nail cutting time. Trim the hair on the footpads. Now your pup is ready for his bath if this is the week it is scheduled. A Havanese brushed regularly will need very few baths. If you set a regular brushing routine of about two or three times a week, you will soon amaze even yourself at how quickly this will go. If done regularly, I find it takes me about 15 to 20 minutes.

16. The last step. Hug your Havanese. Praise him lavishly and play with him for another 15 minutes as his reward.

Finish grooming sessions by combing the face, beard, and head using a medium-tooth comb. Brushes used around the eyes may cause damage if your dog moves unexpectedly.

COAT PROBLEMS

Facts About Matted Hair

All long-haired dogs get mats if they are incorrectly brushed. A common error is to select the right brush for your dog then use it to brush the top coat only and assume that the job is thorough. Instead, this usually results in the dog becoming one solid block of matting next to the skin. Large mats can be difficult to remove, because no dog can be expected to sit quietly while you pull through the coat trying to remove tangles.

There are critical "coat matting" periods for long-haired dogs. The most difficult period is when the dog is about one year of age, and the puppy coat changes to adult mixture. At this time, the top coat is rather sparse, and the hair near the skin is much thicker. If the dog is not brushed every day or every other day, the hair mats together and forms large clumps near the skin that are next to impossible to get out. If the coat is neglected during this critical period, the dog may have to be cut down.

Long periods of damp weather and humidity make the hair mat easily. Winter weather is harsh on long-coated dogs. Pets that are allowed to romp in the snow and become soaking wet tend to mat easily if the coat is not brushed and dried properly afterward.

Brushing Matted Hair

Using a liquid tangle remover, saturate all matted areas and allow the product to remain on the hair until almost dry. Start mat removal by breaking apart large mats and separating them into smaller sections. This can be done with a mat splitter or a rake, a special grooming tool with two rows of diagonally set teeth and rounded ends that will not scratch the dog's skin. After each section is separated, use the brush to start brushing out the mats. When working on damaged or matted hair, always use a protein conditioner between grooming sessions. Rather than just coating the hair with an attractive sheen for a few days, the protein is absorbed into the hair and repairs the damaged hair shaft. The long-term benefits show up after weeks of regular use—the coat builds up strength and is thicker in texture.

Removing Mats from the Show Coat

With a little patience, even the largest mat can be removed from a show coat with little hair loss. The first step is to spray the dog with a protein aerosol conditioner as suggested above or a liquid tangle-removing

preparation. After spraying, work the product into the matted areas with your fingers and allow it to remain on the hair for at least a half hour.

Large mats in show coats should be gently untangled, rather than pulled or cut out. Begin by separating and isolating the mat from the rest of the long coat. Use your fingers to gently work the mat apart and into two smaller sections.

Next, use the mat splitter or rake to break up the two matted sections into four small sections. At this point, the hair needs to be dampened again with the tangle remover. Keep separating each section into small sections, then use a pin or bristle brush to brush out each tiny mat.

Emergency Coat Saving Hints

1. To remove beard and mustache stains or to dry-clean coat: Use a whitener-cleaner. Spray on hair, wait a few minutes, then brush out.

2. To remove grass and underbody stains: Use a whitener-cleaner. Spray on hair, wait about five minutes, then brush out.

3. To remove excessive stains from beards: Saturate stained hair with ginger ale. Let dry, then wash out of hair.

4. To treat itching, scratching, minor skin irritations, insect bites, sunburn, superficial cuts and scratches: Use cortisynth cream or spray affected area with a medicated spray. If irritation is severe or problem

All long-haired dogs will get mats if they are incorrectly brushed. Always brush both the top coat and the undercoat thoroughly to maintain an overall neat appearance. PR Camelot's Spellbinder, owned by Candy Derrick-Houston.

Opposite: Keeping your Havanese well-groomed is important to his health and well-being.

persists, consult a veterinarian.

5. To remove burrs: Saturate burrs with mineral or baby oil. The coat will become slippery and burrs will brush out easily.

6. To remove chewing gum: Rub peanut butter into the gum, let stand a few minutes, then comb out of coat. Another way to remove chewing gum is to rub an ice cube over the gum. It will become brittle and easy to pull out of the hair.

7. To remove grease spots: Use a whitener-cleaner. Dust into coat. Leave on for about an hour, brush out, shampoo and rinse thoroughly. Repeat if necessary.

8. To remove skunk or fertilizer odor: Rub tomato juice or vanilla extract into coat. Leave on for about one hour, then shampoo and rinse thoroughly. Repeat if necessary.

9. To remove tar on feet or coat: Soak tarred area in warm water. Then soak the same area in mineral oil, until the tar loosens and works out of the coat. Or rub vegetable oil into the tarred areas and let it remain in the hair until the tar softens. Shampoo twice and rinse well. Both methods may have to be repeated for stubborn cases.

10. If your dog is chewing his coat: Assuming there is nothing physically wrong with the dog and that he may be chewing out of boredom, spray the hair with bitter-tasting spray or capsicum.

EYE CARE

Most of the long-haired, nonshedding breeds need daily eye care to keep the face from staining. It also seems that the curlier the hair, the greater the risk of staining from eye irritation and tearing.

If your pet tends to have more eye staining than the average dog, there are several things to consider and several steps you can take to help control the problem. Eye stain is caused by many different factors—heredity, teething, improper diet, negligence in grooming, or infection of the tear ducts.

Let us consider each of these causes to help you determine which of these problems might apply to your dog's condition.

Heredity

Many of the Toy breeds inherit small tear ducts. Often, this can be helped by your vet flushing the tear duct with a hollow, soft plastic needle and a dye-filled syringe. This procedure can be done while the pup is under a light anesthesia for teeth cleaning or any

To keep their faces from staining, most long-haired, nonshedding breeds will need daily eye care. Havana's Nina, owned by Mary Ann Gerin.

other minor surgery. This not only cleans and flushes out the tear duct, but to a small extent, helps to open up and stretch the duct. If this is truly an inherited condition, your dog will need daily care, but it is not a great problem and a planned routine takes only a few moments each day.

First, take a very fine flea comb and comb out any foreign matter that has accumulated on the hair on the inside corner of the eye. This, not really the tears, is the staining culprit and therefore must be combed away before the cleaning starts, because you do not want to work this into the coat. If the foreign matter is dried into the fur, you will have to soften it with warm water on a cotton ball before removal. Then take a clean ball of cotton and swab the hair in that area with one of the products on the market today, purchased at any pet shop. Following the swabbing, take a dry cotton ball and wipe away as much of the liquid as possible, flattening the hair down away from the eye. Daily care will improve the condition so much that you will be pleasantly surprised with the results in just days. A word of caution: Some dogs (even though the eye care products claim to be nonallergic and safe) do tend to show an allergic reaction, i.e., swelling of the eyelids, etc. If your dog has any reaction, discontinue use and stick to warm water for cleaning this area. I find the warm water is just as good. The trick is to keep

Use grooming sessions to stay on top of your Havanese's physical condition by checking for bumps, bruises, or parasites. UKC Ch. ZB's Tejas Buckaroo.

their little face clean. The "matter" in the corner is actually bacteria and if allowed to accumulate will start an infection that will scar the tear duct and cause the pup to tear profusely for the remainder of his life.

Teething

Your puppy will naturally tear more during the times that he is teething, and the same daily routine will benefit them greatly. Also at this time, the puppies are playing roughly with each other and the tearing problem can also be caused by hair getting into the eye and irritating the eyes—sometimes a stray hair can actually get on the eyeball. Take your puppy to a window or any place where the light is exceptionally good. Turn his head slowly from side to side as you closely examine the eyeball. If you observe a stray hair lying on the eye itself, gently remove it with a cotton swab. Try to remember that this hair would have been irritating your puppy's eye the same as it would yours, but unlike you, he has no way to remove it for himself. Also, gently pull the lower lid away from the eye and closely observe the well between the inside lid and the eyeball. Often the hair will lodge in this area and must also be removed very gently with a cotton swab.

Improper Diet

Remember the old saying that you get exactly what you pay for? Bargain dog foods are not very often well balanced, and a good, well-balanced food will go a long way in not only keeping your pet in top condition, but his eyes healthy, clear, and bright. By the way, the red dye put into dog food is no more beneficial to your dog than it is to you. It is added to cheaper dog foods as a sales point for humans. When we see the red color, our brain associates this with red meat and subconsciously we feel that the pet is getting more of what he needs, when in reality, just the opposite is correct. The dye is picked up in your dog's system and is expelled through the body's fluids (tears, saliva, urine, and feces) and also stains the hair about the mouth and eyes. Take the label from your dog food and ask your vet to tell you exactly what you are

A well-balanced diet goes a long way in not only keeping your pet in top condition, but also keeps his coat healthy and eyes bright.

feeding your pet. Quite often, harmful additives are so disguised that the average layman has no idea what they really are.

Neglect in Grooming

Neglect in grooming is probably the greatest contributor to the problem of severe staining. For example, matter collecting in the corner of the eye over a period of time will actually cause a large raw spot on the skin, which can contribute to a serious infection. This has been known to cause "cherry eye," which can require surgery to correct.

Infection of the Tear Ducts

This also is a very common problem. If the infection has been present long enough that eye drops do not seem to help, then the infection has probably become systemic and the only thing that will help is an antibiotic. You will notice the difference in the staining in just a matter of days. Continue with the cleaning procedure while treating orally.

Then we come to the last option. It is impossible for me to get my dogs to any shows, so I do not worry about the strict rules for show-ring grooming. I opt to clean the face below the eyes and on the inside corner and also shorten the hair above the eyes in the same manner as their cousin, the Bichon Frise. I don't mean cut it all off—just the inside corner and then, with the clippers, sweep up and out to enable you to see those beautiful eyes.

Our Havanese has such large, expressive eyes that I have often felt it was a shame to hide their beautiful expression behind all that hair. There is an old wives' tale that states if you cut the hair away from the eyes of a long-haired dog that they will go blind, but this has no validity at all. Observe a picture of a dog in a "pet trim" and see how clear the eyes look with the hair taken from around the eyes. Often, trimming the face in this manner will go a long way for controlling the tearing problem, and if you are not taking your dog into the ring, you might consider it. One word of caution: If you trim your dog yourself, never use pointed scissors around the eyes. Also, watch wire and bristle brushes when grooming your dog's head. I prefer a comb when doing the head and little round-nosed scissors for trimming around the eyes. Be careful that you are in excellent light when trimming close to avoid nicking the skin. I hope one or more of these suggestions will help if your pet has a tearing problem.

Opposite: A potential Havanese owner should realize that his long double coat will require considerable grooming to keep it healthy and looking nice. UKC PR Havana's Sophia Jasmine Silk and Carousel's Sydney-Anne , owned by Darnell Phillips.

TRAINING YOUR HAVANESE

I want you to know that I have spent the last 40 years of my life raising dogs, and I have enjoyed almost every minute of it. Over those 40 years, I have learned a great deal about how dogs think, so now I have compiled many of those hints to help you raise a healthy, happy, and well-adjusted dog that will give you many, many years of love and happiness.

YOUR DOG MUST ALWAYS THINK HE IS A SUCCESS

This is the *sine qua non* of dog training. According to research, lack of success is the most common reason why some dogs fail to learn. Even if your dog

Eager to please and highly intelligent, the Havanese can be obedience trained with very little effort.

54

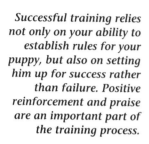

Successful training relies not only on your ability to establish rules for your puppy, but also on setting him up for success rather than failure. Positive reinforcement and praise are an important part of the training process.

gives a seemingly inadequate performance, it is essential that he feels he has done something right—something to merit your praise. More than anything else, he wants your praise.

When your dog has difficulty learning a new lesson, go back and repeat one that he has already mastered. Then you can honestly praise his performance, giving his ego a boost. He'll be ready to try the new lesson again next time.

The social development of your puppy is entirely up to you. A dog is probably the most adaptable pet in the world, but he is also a creature of habit that reacts to the environment provided for him. When an owner says, "My dog won't come when called," or "He can't be housetrained," it is an admission by the owner that he has somehow or somewhere failed his dog. All dogs need praise and this is especially true of the Havanese. He craves approval and cooperates to get it.

You cannot keep your dog confined to an area closed off from the family activity for days on end or tied to a stake in the backyard most of his waking hours without fostering the boredom and frustration that produces a dog that barks, howls, destroys, and maybe soils. It is the best way I know to completely change your puppy's disposition from loving to distrustful. He will become shy and insecure.

It is a rare puppy indeed that is not trusting, loving, and of good nature. Your dog can become as good or as bad, as smart or as stupid as you make him. He needs human companionship, understanding, and socializing to become the dog you expect him to be.

The dog that is a true member of the family is secure and confident and will not often cause trouble. It is through your giving love and companionship to him that he will return it to you tenfold for years to come.

DOG PSYCHOLOGY

Throughout hundreds of years, the dog accomplished such responsible jobs as hunting, sled pulling, and shepherding; he has guarded property, guided the blind, and searched out lost individuals. The dog is highly intelligent and Havanese are exceptionally smart. Training should be an easy job for any dog owner. Show your dog what you want him to do and he will do it.

Dogs are to be cared for, loved, and played with. They are to be walked with, hunted over, trained, exhibited, bragged about, chuckled at, and inevitably mourned. Primarily, they are to be enjoyed. But, between dog and owner there can only be one boss, and the choice is in the hands of the owner. Try always to remember that by being a strong, kind leader your dog will not only respect your wishes, he will love you more.

No one enjoys a tyrant—and no dog need be one—yet far too many dogs are just that. There is the spaniel that must be muzzled and even tranquilized before he can be groomed. There is the terrier that snarls and snaps at anyone who tries to touch him or pick him up, simply because he has discovered he can get away with it. Remember that the only way a dog can get his own way is by growling or snapping.

There is the large dog (or small dog, for that matter) that walks on a leash as though he were a draft horse in a pulling contest. He is probably the most common offender. The moment the leash is snapped on and the front door is opened, he leans into his collar and literally hauls his owner down the sidewalk. It is difficult to determine who is being taken for the walk.

Dog owners benefit from training, too. During obedience training you learn how to establish household rules and how to prevent problem behaviors from occurring—like digging in your garden!

There is the dog that knowingly and deliberately breaks your rules whenever he senses that he can get away with it. While no one is paying particular attention to him, he curls up on the forbidden furniture, snitches food from the table or kitchen counter, and cleans out the cat litter box. He is the nuisance barker, the jumper-upper, and the manipulator that begs effectively at the table. Then there is the dog that threatens the family members with his growls over his food or possessions.

None of these habits are pleasant to live with and certainly none are necessary. They can be forestalled in puppyhood so that they never develop at all or, having developed, can be turned around in all but a very few genuinely difficult cases. The mastery of man over dog is, in fact, very much in keeping with the basic nature of the canine species.

Dogs—all breeds, shapes, and sizes—are pack animals. They always have been. In their wild state, dogs existed in packs built around one leader, the strongest individual among them. Domestication has changed dogs a great deal, but it has not altered this instinct to follow the leader. The only difference is

Teach your Havanese as a puppy what you want him to do as an adult. What he learns in his early months will have bearing on his behavior for the rest of his life. This is eight-week-old Bolero, owned by Vivian Becella.

Opposite: In their wild state, dogs existed in family packs built around one leader. It is important to establish yourself as the pack leader from the beginning of your relationship with your Havanese. Alison Hashmall and Lucia Margherita.

that the domesticated dog attaches himself to a human master rather than a canine leader and takes on his new owner as his leader after he leaves his mother and littermates. Several dogs will live peacefully under one roof because they are the members of the pack, and their owner is the leader.

The reason for the differences and trainability between dogs and cats is that cats do not have this instinct for banding together and adhering to one leader. Dogs are quite the opposite. Their need for a leader persists, but centuries of wild existence have taught them not to entrust themselves to a weak leader. They constantly test the strength of will and the determination of the dog or human who is in the position of leadership. In exactly the same way a four-year-old child tests his parents, a four-month-old puppy watches from the corner of his eye to see what will happen if he tears up the corner of the rug. When he is punished for doing something he knew was forbidden, he feels secure because he knows that he's in the care of a strong leader. Strange as this may sound to you, it is without a doubt a proven fact.

An intelligent and strong-willed dog is quick to sense timidity, an inclination to overindulgent softness, lack of interest, or sometimes outright fear in his owner. Such a dog in the hands of such an owner will not hesitate to take over the position of pack leader, and this is exactly what happens time and again. Bad temperament can be an inherited trait, but in the majority of cases, it is simply the result of inadequate discipline. It seems much easier to blame it on inheritance than to admit that we have failed to hold the position of authority.

Some owners are afraid that their dogs won't love them if they speak to them sternly or discipline them. The fact is that intelligent, consistent discipline inspires respect and thus strengthens a dog's affection rather than diminishes it. Furthermore, only a sharp command will be necessary in the dog's adult life. Being consistent will always be the keynote in training.

Two simple rules will practically guarantee well-behaved dogs: Decide before the training begins what the rules will be, and never let an act of disobedience go uncorrected. Always make direct eye contact when correcting your dog.

Growling and snapping must never be tolerated. It may be natural for a dog to be possessive of his food, his toys, and his share of affection. It may be equally natural for a dog to object to combing, clipping, and nail trimming. However, if a dog is allowed to snarl over his food when a member of the family walks past or snap at the hand that is grooming him, inevitably he will go on from there until he is effectively manipulating everyone in the household. At the first growl or the first lifted lip, scold him in your sternest voice and if it continues, pick him up by the skin over his hips and shoulders, give him a shake, and set him down again. This will not injure him in any way, but most dogs hate it. They feel quite defenseless with their feet off the ground.

Individual dogs vary greatly in the amount of discipline they need. For most, a stern scolding is ample. For others, nothing short of isolation for a period of time from the family will suffice. Just as you would instruct a naughty child to go his your room and don't come out until he is ready to behave properly, put the naughty puppy in his crate and move him to another room where he can spend some "time out" alone. You must judge for yourself what your dog needs. Give him no more, but no less. Spoiled dogs are no more fun to live with than spoiled children, and they are just as unnecessary. Discipline can be and must be a part of the love you give your dog, and it will increase the love and respect he gives to you.

The trick is to control the puppy with love and praise. Always get that eye contact before you correct him or her and be consistent every time. All babies, whether animal or human, learn by repetition. Puppies are babies just learning about life, and for the same reasons that you would not strike a baby, you should never strike your puppy.

POTTY TRAINING MADE FAST AND EASY

Establishing reliable potty habits can be made simple through the use of appropriate housetraining techniques.

No matter how cute, smart, or beautiful our dogs may be, unless they are reliably "potty-trained" all those other wonderful attributes will tend to get overlooked. When you think about it, reliable potty habits are a primary factor that decides how much we integrate our dogs into our lives. All too many

pets are condemned to lives of lonely isolation in the backyard or are taken to the pound because their owners failed to spend the time and effort to housetrain them.

The good news is that potty training does not have to be a hard or long-drawn-out ordeal. It does require some of our time, attention, and consistency. This information will spell out the easiest and quickest way to potty train your little buddy, without the screaming, swatting, nose-pushing negative actions that some people think are necessary to potty train their puppy. We are especially lucky that our job is made easier because the Havanese is such a highly intelligent breed.

STEP 1: Click and Treat Conditioning

It is not essential to develop click and treat communication and reinforcement with your dog in order to potty train him, but it will make things a lot easier and quicker if you do. Click and treat conditioning involves developing the use of a secondary reinforcer. A primary reinforcer is anything that our dog normally wants because it satisfies a basic desire or is basically pleasurable (food, tummy rubs, etc.). A secondary reinforcer is anything that has acquired value by having been paired with a primary reinforcer. The advantage to using a secondary reinforcer is that it enables us to precisely communicate with our dog exactly what aspect of his behavior that we like and wish to have repeated. Without having acquired value by its pairing with a primary reinforcer, a secondary reinforcer is meaningless.

We can begin click and treat conditioning on the first day with a new pup. We need to select a sound that we do not normally make at anytime. I use the tongue-click sound that as kids we associated with imitating the footsteps of a horse. This is a distinctive sound that my dogs only hear when I choose; it can't be confused with the sound of my voice, which they hear all the time.

Next, we turn our sound into a special secondary reinforcer by handfeeding our dog and by making our special sound every time we pop a nugget of food into our pup's mouth.

After a few feeding sessions we begin to make our special sound a split second before we pop the tasty items into the pup's mouth. Gradually, we increase the time between the sound and the tidbit of food to three to five seconds (over several feeding sessions).

When we see our pup perk up his ears, startle, or look around expectantly at the presentation of our special sound, we know that an association has been established and that we can now use that sound as a communication tool to train our buddy more quickly, easily, and positively.

To effectively use click and treat training, it is most helpful to know how much to feed your furry buddy each day in order to maintain optimum health. (Food deprivation is cruel and unhealthy, and is to be

When housetraining your Havanese, reinforce what he has learned by praising him when he relieves himself in the correct area.

avoided at all costs; overfeeding to the point of creating little blimps is also not good for our doggie's health.) Consult with your vet and breeder about the recommended amounts and kinds of food for meals and additional treats. Leaving out a bowl of food all day for our pet to come and go and eat whenever he pleases is not a practice that supports effective training and makes a disastrous guess work of potty training.

STEP 2: Potty-Training Basics

Here's the secret: Potty training requires your 100 percent concentrated efforts for the first few days as you reinforce the pottying behavior that you wish to establish and prevent pottying behaviors in the wrong places.

Begin by entertaining the idea of using a combination of paper training as well as outdoor training. Paper training and outdoor training are totally compatible. With little dogs, it is very easy to maintain a small paper-potty station in an out of the way corner of a laundry room, utility room, or bathroom. I've never found this to be confusing to my dogs, who prefer to go outside for potty purposes, but will use their paper-potty station on those days when I have to work longer than usual. I keep this paper-potty station in my laundry room. It consists of two side-by-side oil-drip pans that are 18 x 24 inches with slightly curled up edges that I bought at an auto parts store. I cover these metal trays with several layers of clean newspaper. This is sufficient for Havanese to use, although they still prefer the backyard.

Totally dedicate a few consecutive days to establishing the basics of potty training with the puppy (a long weekend is probably enough for a solid foundation). If we will commit ourselves completely for a few days, we will reap the benefits for the lifetime of our furry family member.

Do not plan any projects or activities and limit distractions for this period except to be with the puppy all of the time. Of course, have lots of doggie toys available for playtimes.

Opposite: Havanese are creatures of habit and thrive on routine, so to make training easier, set a schedule for eating, eliminating, playing, walking, and sleeping.

If you take your puppy to the same place to eliminate each time, he will know what is expected of him.

Set up an exercise pen on an uncarpeted section of floor that can easily be cleaned and in an area where he can see all the family activity. Exercise pens are usually 4 x 4 inches. Cover the floor of the enclosed space with newspaper at least two layers thick. Get a little crate, equip it with nice soft bedding, and set it in the corner of the ex-pen with its door propped open. A pup won't soil his bedding, and it will make a nice place for naps during the day. It will also introduce the crate to the pup as a pleasant haven just for him. The design of this area is so that when your pup is in the ex-pen, he will either be on newspapers (a permissible potty target) or in his crate, which he innately will avoid soiling.

Have the pup's food rations (for meals and treats) easily available for you to use as a training aid.

Be aware that puppies most frequently will need to urinate and defecate upon awakening, after eating, after drinking, and after playing. Clues that pottying behavior is imminent often include sniffing the ground, walking in little circles, and walking with a slightly arched back. These times and clues, while pretty reliable, will have some variations with each individual pup, so it is imperative that you spend these

There are two absolutely essential items that all pups must learn: to come when called and to be reliably housetrained.

few days being a good observer of your new little family member.

To make the most of our time, our goal is to be on hand each and every time our pup potties during these few days so that we can direct and reinforce exactly what we want. We'll be alternating our puppy's playtimes and rest times. Open the ex-pen during the playtime so that the puppy can enter or leave the papered area. As we play with our pup, we'll be watching him every second and be alert for any change in his behavior; a few sniffs can quickly trigger a "squat," so we must be ready to get the pup to the newspaper before a dribble begins. Ideally, after every few minutes of playing, we should guide the pup to the papered area and say whatever word we've chosen to mean "potty" for our little buddy. Often, nothing will happen, but we need to be patient and give the pup time to act; if we get the desired performance on the newspaper, we click, treat, and praise, praise, praise!

If our pup goes into a squat without being over the paper, we immediately say, "No!" in a serious voice. Then, as rapidly as possible, we lift and transport the pup to the newspaper where we can encourage pottying in the proper place. Eventually, the puppy will resume the pottying behavior, giving us a chance to click and treat and oooh and aaah!

The pattern of taking the puppy to the newspapered area every few minutes during play and immediately after napping, eating, or drinking will maximize our opportunities for success. With each success, it is critical that we communicate our pleasure as accurately as possible. Clicking as the pup finishes pottying and following the click with treats, lots of praise, and affection pinpoints for the pup that action which is responsible for the positive reinforcement.

This initial period of time helps us establish expectations and routines by setting up an absolutely consistent effort. We'll need to keep reinforcing good potty behavior and preventing mistakes. Preventing mistakes means continuing to have a safe place for the pup to be when we aren't actually interacting with him.

Incorporating outside pottying is an easy and natural next step. The key is to take, not send, your pup outside. Only by taking him out can you reinforce the behavior you seek.

The success of this job is really up to you. The

young puppy must be taken out every few hours and always the very first thing in the morning. Carry him out from his bed or pen after each meal, after exciting play, just before putting him to bed at night, after naps, and of course, several times in between just for good measure so that he has no chance to squat before he's outdoors. Any time that he appears restless and noses about, pick him up and take him out immediately. If you use the same door every time, he'll eventually learn to go there when he wants to go out. Always keep him out long enough. Don't rush him and don't just put him out alone. Take him to the area that you expect him to use. A dog is a creature of habit, and once forming the habit to go in one spot he can be counted on to return each time to the spot that you have selected for him. Be sure to praise him warmly on "mission accomplished." It is the nature of dogs to want to please those they love and there is nothing like praise and petting to teach them what we wish for them to learn. I hope that you will forgive my repetition on this point, but I cannot tell you how strongly I feel on the subject to reward instead of punishment in discipline whenever possible. This makes for a happy, loving, self-assured, and obedient dog. He then will be a true joy and full member of the family.

The old practice of rubbing the pup's nose in his or her mistake is absolutely gross and teaches the dog nothing more than how to avoid getting caught.

PUPPY TRAINING

There are two absolutely essential items that pups must learn: to come when called and be reliably housetrained. There is a third critical component that all pups need to learn and that is to behave cooperatively when being handled.

There are several specific handling objectives to be taught: 1. Foot Handling; 2. Mouth Handling; 3. Ear Handling; and 4. Brushing.

The basic principles for teaching our pups to allow us to touch sensitive areas are these:

1. Begin with very brief, gentle, simple touches and progress systematically by gradually increasing the time length of the touch or the amount or complexity of handling that the touch entails.

2. Proceed to the next longer or more complex level of touch *only* after your current level of touch is consistently accepted calmly and politely.

You must be able to care for your dog, which means your Havanese should calmly permit you to handle his feet, mouth, ears, and tail.

3. Practice the current touch-step several times daily. (It should only take a few seconds.)

4. Reinforce successful acceptance of the touch by praising, clicking, and treating. Click and treat training is by far the easiest way to accustom any pup or dog to these handling maneuvers. It allows precise communication with your furry buddy about exactly which instance of behavior is being reinforced.

5. Speak reassuringly with a happy calm voice (not a sympathetic voice) as the touch is practiced.

6. If you have difficulty at any phase of developing sensitive touch-acceptance, back down the level of touch-complexity or touch-length being requested to a simpler phase at which success was easily obtained. Then break down the behavioral touch-acceptance steps into finer increments. Remember to praise, click, and treat at each little step!

Foot handling, mouth handling, and ear handling require similar techniques, which should be performed on our new puppy several times daily while he is learning to accept them. (If your dog is beyond puppy training and still hasn't been taught to allow handling of these areas, we can still teach them. It's never too late if we persist and are consistent.)

Foot Handling Steps

Do each step with all four feet, one at a time, at each practice session.

1. Gently touch the puppy's paws while petting him. A single light touch with fingertips is the safest way to start.

2. Gently take a paw in your hand and hold it lightly for a couple seconds.

3. Hold a paw gently in one hand and very lightly stroke the top of the foot (the furry part, not the pad) with the other hand.

4. Hold the foot with one hand and use one or two fingers of the other hand to gently stroke each individual toe from base to tip.

5. Hold the foot with one hand and use the thumb and index finger of the other hand to gently hold each toenail.

6. Hold the foot with one hand and use the thumb and index finger of the other hand to gently and briefly massage down each individual toe and toenail from base to tip.

7. Hold the foot with one hand and use the toenail

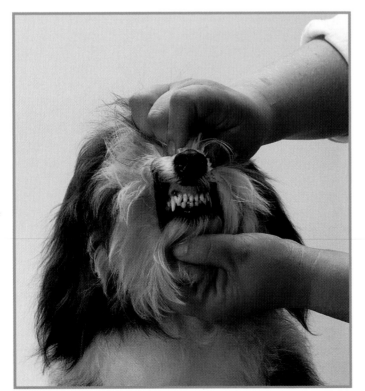

Proper mouth handling is necessary for maintaining oral hygiene, as well as for administering medications if ever needed.

clippers with the other hand to gently touch each toenail tip once. If your furry friend has had an unpleasant experience with toenail clippers, just place the clippers within view of the dog and proceed again with steps one through six.

8. Hold the foot with one hand and use the toenail clippers to make "pretend" nail cuts — go through the motions of handling each toenail and barely slip each toenail into place in the clipper, but don't clip yet.

9. Hold the foot with one hand and use the clippers to snip a miniscule amount off each nail. It will probably take a few weeks to reach this phase, but once you have, you will be able to easily snip tiny bits of nail off daily. Be patient. Don't rush and get overly zealous about taking off too much nail at once.

Mouth Handling Steps

This is necessary for oral hygiene (teeth brushing), as well as for administering medications if ever needed.

1. Place one hand under the pup's chin and use the other hand to pet each side of the muzzle very gently.

2. Play peek-a-boo with the pup's front-lateral teeth (the canines) by gently sliding both sides of the upper lip up (one at a time), and both sides of the lower lip down (one at a time).

3. Gradually prolong the peek-a-boo postures of the lips until your furry buddy calmly accepts about five seconds in each of the four positions.

4. While playing peek-a-boo with the canine teeth (one at a time), gently slide the fingers back that are pushing the upper lip up (and then the fingers that are pulling the lower lip down) so that teeth farther back in the mouth than the canine teeth are exposed. Gradually prolong the time that the pup is asked to accept having his lip gently pulled up, down, and backward to about five seconds.

6. With one hand supporting the dog's head, gently use the thumb of the same hand for pulling the lip up or down. Meanwhile, using the index finger of the other hand, softly and briefly touch the canine tooth.

7. Gradually increase how far back toward the corners of the mouth the pup accepts the combined lip moving and tooth touching until any tooth in the mouth can be very briefly touched.

8. Gradually prolong the length of time that the lip positioning and tooth touching are accepted to about five seconds.

9. Introduce a soft, bristled, child-sized or official doggie toothbrush and doggie toothpaste. Put doggie

toothpaste on the brush and show it to the pup, allowing him or her to lick it off.

10. After the dog is convinced that the toothbrush and doggie toothpaste are good things, gently touch a canine tooth for a very brief instant with the bristled end of the brush.

11. Gradually increase the number of teeth that can be touched with the toothbrush. This may take several quick sessions daily for several days.

12. When each tooth can be touched easily for about five seconds gently and quickly, make a single brush stroke on the canine teeth (one at a time of course). Gradually increase the number of teeth on which a single brush stroke can be performed. At first, it's safest to only make the brush stroke on one or two teeth per session.

Once the dog calmly accepts teeth brushing, it will be much easier to do the handling necessary for administering medications. If it is necessary to do this, any good vet should be able to demonstrate the easiest hand position that is useful for large capsules. Liquid medication will also be far easier to administer using a syringe inserted into the side of the dog's

Use only as much correction as is needed to get your dog's attention and remember to correct only when he makes a mistake, not after.

Opposite: Training your Havanese is a learning process that requires time, patience, and dedication.

mouth and "triggered" slowly so that only a drop or two goes into the dog's mouth to be swallowed at a time. Whenever possible, however, I like to just "sneak" the medicine into something tasty like cheese or a hot dog.

Ear Handling

This is easy. It simply involves gently holding our dog's ears one at a time and briefly touching the underside of the outer ear while we're petting them so that they get used to having their ears manipulated.

It is critical to realize that during the training of any of these handling-acceptance exercises not much, if anything, in the way of grooming will be accomplished. The goal is to establish a trusting bond and calm acceptance of our handling so that eventually we can accomplish whatever is needed easily, without struggle and frazzled nerves for either the two-legged or four-legged member of the duo.

SOME GENERAL RULES FOR TRAINING YOUR HAVANESE

Praise a dog when he merits it and scold him when he disobeys. Stick to the same set of words when praising or disapproving and to the same tones of voice. Decide upon a word like "good," "fine," or "okay," and stay with it. Decide the same for disapproval and get eye contact when scolding. A dog understands the tone of voice and your stern face better than words. If you say "shame" to him in a sweet voice, he will misunderstand you and think you are encouraging him. Conversely, when you call him a "bum," don't smile.

Always show a dog what you want him to do. If you want him to sit in a certain chair, put him in it and say "chair" to him over and over. Repeat this procedure and after a while, start scolding him if he jumps off. Praise him if he stays put. After a short time, he should know what "sit in the chair" means.

Don't scold a dog for a mistake he has made sometime before, and never call a dog to you to punish him; eventually, he won't come to you. Go after him! Never allow him to associate the calling of his name to come to you with the discipline he is about to incur.

Lead Breaking

When teaching a dog to walk on a lead (leash), first clip it on his collar and let him drag it around a bit to see that it will not hurt him. Take this step gradually,

At first, your puppy may be annoyed by a leash and collar, but eventually he will learn to ignore it. Your Havanese must learn to accept the leash for his safety and the safety of others.

because he will fight the lead at first, so just a little at a time is a good idea. Then pick up the lead, and while still facing him, gently tug and encourage him to come along with you. Never leave his collar on him when you are not with him when he is small, as it is possible for it to catch on something and hang him. Puppies are very curious and poke their little head into all sorts of openings.

Heeling

A dog that pulls on a leash or zigzags across the sidewalk is a nuisance and should be taught to stay at the owner's side. Training your dog to heel should begin in the house. Walk with the dog on a short leash, and when he is at your side, praise him and say "heel" or "back." Slacken the leash. If he goes ahead, scold him and pull him back. The dog should always be on your left side. I have heard many trainers advise starting out with a little harness on a small puppy rather than a collar. However, jerking their neck to bring them back to the heel position can cause future problems with their larynx.

Jumping on People

If you want to break your Havanese of this habit,

scold him every single time he lifts his front feet off the floor. The very best way to stop this behavior is to use the "sit" command. This is the reason I stress teaching the sit command almost as soon as you get your little one settled in and to keep rewarding and reinforcing this procedure.

Biting or Nipping

A puppy should have his own toys, and he should learn that he is permitted to chew on these things. Be stern about not letting him chew objects like furniture, rugs, shoes, etc. Also, with a puppy that already shows a bit of aggression, don't play tug-of-war with him. It tends to make him more competitive.

The best way to break a puppy from nipping is to substitute play for this habit. When he comes toward you looking as if he might nip, reach out to pet him and give him a toy. If he persists, scold him, looking him in the eyes, and send him to his bed. An older puppy that starts this unpleasant habit may take a little more firm discipline. When he nips, wrap your hand around his muzzle and squeeze, saying harshly, "No." Then continue to play with the puppy so that he will learn that it is not the playing that you disapprove of but the nipping. If he still persists, wrap your hand around his muzzle and with the heel of the other hand, gently bump the end of his nose, again saying, "No." When bumping his nose, remember to go easy, because he is just a baby and you only need the "bump" enough to make him feel discomfort, not pain. Then continue to play as before. Be consistent about this. If it is not stopped in the beginning, it can develop into a serious habit. Puppies usually nip in the excitement of play or for attention, but never let him get away with it.

Excessive Barking

Dogs that bark every time they hear a slight noise are nervous dogs. Nip this habit when the dog is a puppy. If he barks at slight noises, don't scold him, reassure him. You want your dog to alarm you in case of danger, but an excessive barker is a nuisance to everyone. Dogs that bark when they are left alone are problems, too. To avoid this, start when the dog is young. Put him in a room by himself at first for short periods and gradually lengthen the period to get him accustomed to staying by himself. Always see to it that he has his chew toys to entertain himself. Bored puppies are destructive puppies.

If your dog barks when someone comes to the door, allow him to bark three or four times then pick the pup up in your arms. As you approach the door, say "hush" firmly but gently. The idea to get across to your pup is that he has done his job and now you will take over. Hold the pup in your arms until the visitor is inside. Place the pup on the floor and command him firmly to sit.

Being taught good manners and obedience skills can help ensure that your Havanese will become a treasured family member for years to come. Havana Wiley, owned by Maxine Polansky.

Obedience Classes

Over the years obedience classes have sprung up all over the country. The kind sponsored in most cities by local civic clubs, where attendance fees are negligible, use advanced amateurs and professionals to train the dogs. Their goal is to improve the manners and social graces of all dogs. NEVER allow a trainer to use force that you feel is cruel in any way with your dog. Do not hesitate nor feel embarrassed to tell a trainer to stop if your puppy is being frightened. Trainers do not know everything. This is your puppy and trainers come in all degrees of expertise. More widely known and more reliable are the obedience clubs run by local groups under the eye of the American Kennel Club (AKC). These groups charge a slightly higher though still nominal fee.

YOUR HEALTHY
HAVANESE

Dogs, like all other animals, are capable of contracting problems and diseases that, in most cases, are easily avoided by sound husbandry—meaning well-bred and well-cared-for animals are less prone to developing diseases and problems than are carelessly bred and neglected animals. Your knowledge of how to avoid problems is far more valuable than all of the books and advice on how to cure them. Respectively, the only person you should listen to about treatment is your vet. Veterinarians don't have all the answers, but at least they are trained to analyze and treat illnesses, and are aware of the full implications of treatments. This does not mean a few old remedies aren't good standbys when all else fails, but in most cases modern science provides the best treatments for disease.

PHYSICAL EXAMS

Your puppy should receive regular physical examinations or checkups. These come in two forms. One is obviously performed by your vet, and the other is a day-to-day procedure that should be done by you. Apart from the fact the exam will highlight any problem at an early stage, it is an excellent way of socializing the pup to being handled.

To do the physical exam yourself, start at the head and work your way around the body. You are looking for any sign of lesions, or any indication of parasites on the pup. The most common parasites are fleas and ticks.

HEALTHY TEETH AND GUMS

Chewing is instinctual. Puppies chew so that their teeth and jaws grow strong and healthy as they develop. As the permanent teeth begin to emerge, it is painful and annoying to the puppy, and puppy owners must

Opposite: As a responsible Havanese owner, you should have a basic understanding of the medical problems that affect the breed.

78

Healthy teeth and gums are important to the well-being of your Havanese. Check and brush his teeth regularly—this is especially important with Toy breeds.

recognize that their new charges need something safe upon which to chew. Unfortunately, once the puppy's permanent teeth have emerged and settled solidly into the jaw, the chewing instinct does not fade. Adult dogs instinctively need to clean their teeth, massage their gums, and exercise their jaws through chewing.

It is necessary for your dog to have clean teeth. You should take your dog to the veterinarian at least once a year to have his teeth cleaned and to have his mouth examined for any sign of oral disease. Although dogs do not get cavities in the same way humans do, dogs' teeth accumulate tartar, and more quickly than humans do! Veterinarians recommend brushing your dog's teeth daily. But who can find time to brush their dog's teeth daily? The accumulation of tartar and plaque on our dog's teeth when not removed can cause irritation and eventually erode the enamel and finally destroy the teeth. Advanced cases, while destroying the teeth, bring on gingivitis and periodontitis, two very serious conditions that can affect the dog's internal organs as well...to say nothing about bad breath!

Since everyone can't brush their dog's teeth daily or get to the veterinarian often enough for him to scale the dog's teeth, providing the dog with something safe to chew on will help maintain oral hygiene. Chew devices from Nylabone® keep dogs' teeth clean, but they also provide an excellent resource for entertainment and relief of doggie tensions. Nylabone® products give your dog something to do for an hour or two every day and during that hour or two, your dog will be taking an active part in keeping his teeth and gums healthy...without even realizing it! That's invaluable to your dog, and valuable to you!

Nylabone® provides fun bones, challenging bones, and *safe* bones. It is an owner's responsibility to recognize safe chew toys from dangerous ones. Your dog will chew and devour anything you give him. Dogs must not be permitted to chew on items that they can break. Pieces of broken objects can do internal damage to a dog, besides ripping the dog's mouth. Cheap plastic or rubber toys can cause stoppage in the intestines; such stoppages are operable only if caught immediately.

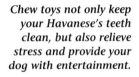

Chew toys not only keep your Havanese's teeth clean, but also relieve stress and provide your dog with entertainment.

The most obvious choices, in this case, may be the worst choice. Natural beef bones were not designed for chewing and cannot take too much pressure from

the sides. Due to the abrasive nature of these bones, they should be offered most sparingly. Knuckle bones, though once very popular for dogs, can be easily chewed up and eaten by dogs. At the very least, digestion is interrupted; at worst, the dog can choke or suffer from intestinal blockage.

When a dog chews hard on a Nylabone®, little bristle-like projections appear on the surface of the bone. These help to clean the dog's teeth and add to the gum-massaging. Given the chemistry of the nylon, the bristle can pass through the dog's intestinal tract without effect. Since nylon is inert, no microorganism can grow on it, and it can be washed in soap and water or sterilized in boiling water or in an autoclave.

For the sake of your dog, his teeth, and your own peace of mind, provide your dog with Nylabones®. They have 100 variations from which to choose.

FIGHTING FLEAS

Fleas are very mobile and may be red, black, or brown in color. The adults suck the blood of the host, while the larvae feed on the feces of the adults, which is rich in blood. Flea "dirt" may be seen on the pup as very tiny clusters of blackish specks that look

There are many parasites, like fleas and ticks, that your dog may encounter when playing outside. Be sure to check your Havanese's coat thoroughly when he comes in from the outdoors. Pablo Ricky De ZB's, owned by Angela Houston.

Regular physical examinations are vital to the health and long life of your canine companion.

like freshly ground pepper. The eggs of fleas may be laid on the puppy, though they are more commonly laid off the host in a favorable place, such as the bedding. They normally hatch in 4 to 21 days, depending on the temperature, but they can survive for up to 18 months if temperature conditions are not favorable. The larvae are maggot-like and molt a couple of times before forming pupae, which can survive long periods until the temperature, or the vibration of a nearby host, causes them to emerge and jump on a host.

There are a number of effective treatments available, and you should discuss them with your veterinarian, then follow all instructions for the one you choose. Any treatment will involve a product for your puppy or dog and one for the environment, and will require diligence on your part to treat all areas and thoroughly clean your home and yard until the infestation is eradicated.

THE TROUBLE WITH TICKS

Ticks are arthropods of the spider family, which means they have eight legs (though the larvae have six). They bury their headparts into the host and gorge on its blood. They are easily seen as small grain-like creatures sticking out from the skin. They are often picked up when dogs play in fields, but may also arrive in your yard via wild animals—even birds—or stray cats and dogs. Some ticks are species-specific, others are more adaptable and will host on many species.

The most troublesome type of tick is the deer tick, which spreads the deadly Lyme disease that can cripple a dog (or a person). Deer ticks are tiny and very hard to detect. Often, by the time they're big enough to notice, they've been feeding on the dog for a few days—long enough to do their damage. Lyme disease was named for the area of the United States in which it was first detected—Lyme, Connecticut—but has now been diagnosed in almost all parts of the US. Your veterinarian can advise you of the danger to your dog(s) in your area, and may suggest your dog be vaccinated for Lyme. Always go over your dog with a fine-toothed flea comb when you come in from walking through any area that may harbor deer ticks, and if your dog is acting unusually sluggish or sore, seek veterinary advice.

Attempts to pull a tick free will invariably leave the headpart in the pup, where it will die and cause an

All dogs have off days when they do not seem themselves. However, if this lethargic condition persists, you should have your Havanese examined by a professional. Annie, owned by Darnell Phillips.

infected wound or abscess. The best way to remove ticks is to dab a strong saline solution, iodine, or alcohol on them. This will numb them, causing them to loosen their hold, at which time they can be removed with forceps. The wound can then be cleaned and covered with an antiseptic ointment. If ticks are common in your area, consult with your vet for a suitable pesticide to be used in kennels, on bedding, and on the puppy or dog.

INSECTS AND OTHER OUTDOOR DANGERS

There are many biting insects, such as mosquitoes, that can cause discomfort to a puppy. Many diseases are transmitted by the males of these species.

A pup can easily get a grass seed or thorn lodged between his pads or in the folds of his ears. These may go unnoticed until an abscess forms.

This is where your daily check of the puppy or dog will do a world of good. If your puppy has been playing in long grass or places where there may be thorns, pine needles, wild animals, or parasites, the checkup is a wise precaution.

SKIN DISORDERS

Apart from problems associated with lesions created by biting pests, a puppy may fall foul to a number of other skin disorders. Examples are ringworm, mange, and eczema. Ringworm is not caused by a worm, but is a fungal infection. It manifests itself as a sore-looking bald circle. If your puppy should have any form of bald patches, let your veterinarian check him over; a microscopic examination can confirm the condition. Many old remedies for ringworm exist, such as iodine, carbolic acid, formalin, and other tinctures, but modern drugs are superior.

Fungal infections can be very difficult to treat, and even more difficult to eradicate, because of the spores. These can withstand most treatments, other than burning, which is the best thing to do with bedding once the condition has been confirmed.

Mange is a general term that can be applied to many skin conditions where the hair falls out and a flaky crust develops and falls away.

Often, dogs will scratch themselves, and this invariably is worse than the original condition, for it opens lesions that are then subject to viral, fungal, or parasitic attack. The cause of the problem can be various species of mites. These either live on skin debris and the hair follicles, which they destroy, or they bury themselves just beneath the skin and feed on the tissue. Applying general remedies from pet stores is not recommended because it is essential to identify the type of mange before a specific treatment is effective.

Eczema is another nonspecific term applied to many skin disorders. The condition can be brought about in many ways. Sunburn, chemicals, allergies to foods, drugs, pollens, and even stress can all produce a deterioration of the skin and coat. Given the range of causal factors, treatment can be difficult because the problem is one of identification. It is a case of taking each possibility at a time and trying to correctly diagnose the matter. If the cause is of a dietary nature then you must remove one item at a time in order to find out if the dog is allergic to a given food. It could, of course, be the lack of a nutrient that is the problem, so if the condition persists, you should consult your veterinarian.

INTERNAL DISORDERS

It cannot be overstressed that it is very foolish to attempt to diagnose an internal disorder without the advice of a veterinarian. Take a relatively common

The importance of consulting a veterinarian on the diagnosis of internal disorders cannot be overemphasized—a relatively common problem, like diarrhea, could also be a sign of something more serious. Pip, owned by Jennifer Clark.

problem such as diarrhea. It might be caused by nothing more serious than the puppy hogging a lot of food or eating something that it has never previously eaten. Conversely, it could be the first indication of a potentially fatal disease. It's up to your veterinarian to make the correct diagnosis.

The following symptoms, especially if they accompany each other or are progressively added to earlier symptoms, mean you should visit the veterinarian right away:

Continual vomiting. All dogs vomit from time to time and this is not necessarily a sign of illness. They will eat grass to induce vomiting. It is a natural cleansing process common to many carnivores. However, continued vomiting is a clear sign of a problem. It may be a blockage in the pup's intestinal tract, it may be induced by worms, or it could be due to any number of diseases.

Diarrhea. This, too, may be nothing more than a temporary condition due to many factors. Even a change of home can induce diarrhea, because this often stresses the pup, and invariably there is some change in the diet. If it persists more than 48 hours then something is amiss. If blood is seen in the feces, waste no time at all in taking the dog to the vet.

Running eyes and/or nose. A pup might have a chill and this will cause the eyes and nose to weep. Again, this should quickly clear up if the puppy is placed in a warm environment and away from any drafts. If it does not, and especially if a mucous discharge is seen, then the pup has an illness that must be diagnosed.

Coughing. Prolonged coughing is a sign of a problem, usually of a respiratory nature.

Wheezing. If the pup has difficulty breathing and makes a wheezing sound when breathing, then something is wrong.

Cries when attempting to defecate or urinate. This might only be a minor problem due to the hard state of the feces, but it could be more serious, especially if the pup cries when urinating.

Cries when touched. Obviously, if you do not handle a puppy with care he might yelp. However, if he cries even when lifted gently, then he has an internal problem that becomes apparent when pressure is applied to a given area of the body. Clearly, this must be diagnosed.

Refuses food. Generally, puppies and dogs are

greedy creatures when it comes to feeding time. Some might be more fussy, but none should refuse more than one meal. If they go for a number of hours without showing any interest in their food, then something is not as it should be.

General listlessness. All puppies have their off days when they do not seem their usual cheeky, mischievous selves. If this condition persists for more than two days then there is little doubt of a problem. They may not show any of the signs listed, other than perhaps a reduced interest in their food. There are many diseases that can develop internally without displaying obvious clinical signs. Blood, fecal, and other tests are needed in order to identify the disorder before it reaches an advanced state that may not be treatable.

WORMS

There are many species of worms, and a number of these live in the tissues of dogs and most other animals. Many create no problem at all, so you are not even aware they exist. Others can be tolerated in small levels, but become a major problem if they number more than a few. The most common types seen in dogs are roundworms and tapeworms. While roundworms are the greater problem, tape-

Make an appointment with your vet if your Havanese's behavior changes. For example, a loss of interest in food or persistent crying can indicate a health problem.

If your Havanese becomes ill or sustains an injury, acting quickly and appropriately can save his life. Havana's Smoky Mountain Christiana, owned by Barbara Bogart.

worms require an intermediate host so are more easily eradicated.

Roundworms of the species *Toxocara canis* infest the dog. They may grow to a length of 8 inches (20 cm) and look like strings of spaghetti. The worms feed on the digesting food in the pup's intestines. In chronic cases the puppy will become pot-bellied, have diarrhea, and will vomit. Eventually, he will stop eating, having passed through the stage when he always seems hungry. The worms lay eggs in the puppy and these pass out in his feces. They are then either ingested by the pup, or they are eaten by mice, rats, or beetles. These may then be eaten by the puppy and the life cycle is complete.

Larval worms can migrate to the womb of a pregnant bitch, or to her mammary glands, and this is how they pass to the puppy. The pregnant bitch can be wormed, which will help. The pups can, and should, be wormed when they are about two weeks old. Repeat worming every 10 to 14 days and the parasites should be removed. Worms can be extremely dangerous to young puppies, so you should be sure the pup is wormed as a matter of routine.

Tapeworms can be seen as tiny rice-like eggs sticking to the puppy's or dog's anus. They are less destructive, but still undesirable. The eggs are eaten by mice, fleas, rabbits, and other animals that serve as intermediate hosts. They develop into a larval stage and the host must be eaten by the dog in order to complete the chain. Your vet will supply a suitable remedy if tapeworms are seen or suspected. There are other worms, such as hookworms and whipworms, that are also blood suckers. They will make a pup anemic, and blood might be seen in the feces, which can be examined by the vet to confirm their presence. Cleanliness in all matters is the best preventative measure for all worms.

Heartworm infestation in dogs is passed by mosquitoes but can be prevented by a monthly (or daily) treatment that is given orally. Talk to your vet about the risk of heartworm in your area.

BLOAT (GASTRIC DILATATION)

This condition has proved fatal in many dogs, especially large and deep-chested breeds, such as the Weimaraner and the Great Dane. However, any dog can get bloat. It is caused by swallowing air during exercise, food/water gulping or another strenuous task. As many believe, it is not the result of flatulence. The stomach of an affected dog twists, disallowing food and blood flow and resulting in harmful toxins being released into the bloodstream. Death can easily follow if the condition goes undetected.

The best preventative measure is not to feed large meals or exercise your puppy or dog immediately after he has eaten. Veterinarians recommend feeding three smaller meals per day in an elevated feeding rack, adding water to dry food to prevent gulping, and not offering water during mealtimes.

VACCINATIONS

Every puppy, purebred or mixed breed, should be vaccinated against the major canine diseases. These are distemper, leptospirosis, hepatitis, and canine parvovirus. Your puppy may have received a temporary vaccination against distemper before you purchased him, but be sure to ask the breeder to be sure.

The age at which vaccinations are given can vary, but will usually be when the pup is 8 to 12 weeks old. By this time any protection given to the pup by antibodies received from his mother via her initial milk feeds will be losing their strength.

The puppy's immune system works on the basis that the white blood cells engulf and render harmless attacking bacteria. However, they must first recognize a potential enemy.

Vaccines are either dead bacteria or they are live, but in very small doses. Either type prompts the pup's defense system to attack them. When a large attack then comes (if it does), the immune system recognizes it and massive numbers of lymphocytes (white blood corpuscles) are mobilized to counter the attack. However, the ability of the cells to recognize these dangerous viruses can diminish over a period of time. It is therefore useful to provide annual reminders about the nature of the enemy. This is done by means of booster injections that keep the immune system on its alert. Immunization is not 100-percent guaranteed to be successful, but is very close. Certainly it is better than giving the puppy no protection.

Dogs are subject to other viral attacks, and if these are of a high-risk factor in your area, then your vet will suggest you have the puppy vaccinated against these as well.

At 8 to 12 weeks of age, the immunity your puppy received from his mother is wearing off and he'll need to develop his own protection against contagious canine diseases. Rely on your vet for the most effectual vaccination schedule.

Your puppy or dog should also be vaccinated against the deadly rabies virus. In fact, in many places it is illegal for your dog not to be vaccinated. This is to protect your dog, your family, and the rest of the animal population from this deadly virus that infects the nervous system and causes dementia and death.

ACCIDENTS

All puppies will get their share of bumps and bruises due to the rather energetic way they play. These will usually heal themselves over a few days. Small cuts should be bathed with a suitable disinfectant and then smeared with an antiseptic ointment. If a cut looks more serious, then stem the flow of blood with a towel or makeshift tourniquet and rush the pup to the veterinarian. Never apply so much pressure to the wound that it might restrict the flow of blood to the limb.

Opposite: Your Havanese will be a valued member of the family for a long time, so you'll want to ensure that he enjoys good health and a quality lifestyle. Havana's Cinder, owned by John and Sharon Shearman.

In the case of burns you should apply cold water or an ice pack to the surface. If the burn was due to a chemical, then this must be washed away with copious amounts of water. Apply petroleum jelly, or any vegetable oil, to the burn. Trim away the hair if need be. Wrap the dog in a blanket and rush him to the vet. The pup may go into shock, depending on the severity of the burn, and this will result in a lowered blood pressure, which is dangerous and the reason the pup must receive immediate veterinary attention.

If a broken limb is suspected then try to keep the animal as still as possible. Wrap your pup or dog in a blanket to restrict movement and get him to the veterinarian as soon as possible. Do not move the dog's head so it is tilting backward, as this might result in blood entering the lungs.

Do not let your pup jump up and down from heights, as this can cause considerable shock to the joints. Like all youngsters, puppies do not know when enough is enough, so you must do all their thinking for them.

Provided you apply strict hygiene to all aspects of raising your puppy, and you make daily checks on his physical state, you have done as much as you can to safeguard him during his most vulnerable period. Routine visits to your veterinarian are also recommended, especially while the puppy is under one year of age. The vet may notice something that did not seem important to you.

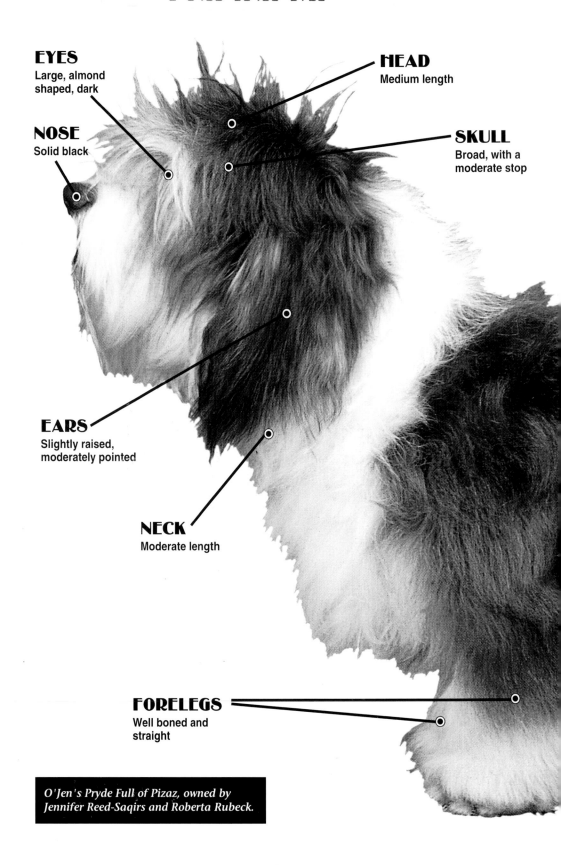

2 1982 00908 6723

EYES
Large, almond shaped, dark

NOSE
Solid black

HEAD
Medium length

SKULL
Broad, with a moderate stop

EARS
Slightly raised, moderately pointed

NECK
Moderate length

FORELEGS
Well boned and straight

O'Jen's Pryde Full of Pizaz, owned by Jennifer Reed-Saqirs and Roberta Rubeck.